Praise for
The Levity Effect

The Levity Effect is no laughing matter. It's a serious work of nonfiction about the powerful influence of laughter and lightness on organizational performance and personal health. While authors Gostick and Christopher entertain us with humorous anecdotes, they also educate us with research, evidence, real-life examples, and practical applications. *The Levity Effect* will have a lasting impact on how you lead.

> —Jim Kouzes, author of
> *The Leadership Challenge*

I absolutely loved this book; as I work with teams around the globe, I have found that this is truly a universal message. Levity is common sense that is uncommonly practiced. This book has been needed for years.

> —Stephan Mardyks, President,
> International, Franklin Covey

A book that proves the theory that you can work hard, reach impressive goals, and still have fun doing it. A humorous, practical guide, filled with real-life examples of what works and what doesn't. And told in a way that grabs you from page one, makes you laugh along the way, and teaches at the same time.

> —Eric J. Lange, Senior Vice President,
> Human Resources, The Nielsen Company

What may be the most valuable business book of the year. From the benefits of chattering teeth awards to the negative effects of jaw clenchers and brow knitters, *The Levity Effect* can change the way you look at corporate culture. Gostick and Christopher have done us all a great service by writing this wonderful book about the power of laughter in the workplace.

—Joe Calloway, author of
Work Like You're Showing Off!

These are serious times. That's why the message of *The Levity Effect* is much needed. The skills for using levity appropriately, and the benefits for doing so, are clearly explained in this enjoyable book. It will help you and your team better enjoy the journey.

—Mark Sanborn, author of *The Fred Factor*

Wow! The funniest, most original business book in ages. With persuasive research and case studies from the least likely businesses, Gostick and Christopher show how any leader can create a competitive advantage by becoming more fun and engaging.

—Chester Elton, *New York Times*
best selling author of *The Invisible Employee*

Lighten up leaders! Work can be fun and enjoyable. In fact, it should be. Engaging your employees in a positive environment is the secret to good (and profitable) business.

—Jon Gordon, author of *The Energy Bus*

THE LEVITY EFFECT

Why It Pays to Lighten Up

Adrian Gostick
and Scott Christopher

WILEY

JOHN WILEY & SONS, INC.

Published by John Wiley & Sons, Inc., Hoboken, New Jersey.

Published simultaneously in Canada.

For general information on our other products and services or for technical support, please contact our Customer Care Department within the United States at (800) 762-2974, outside the United States at (317) 572-3993 or fax (317) 572-4002.

Wiley also publishes its books in a variety of electronic formats. Some content that appears in print may not be available in electronic books. For more information about Wiley products, visit our web site at www.wiley.com.

Library of Congress Cataloging-in-Publication Data:

Gostick, Adrian Robert.
  The levity effect : why it pays to lighten up / Adrian Gostick and Scott Christopher.
      p.   cm.
  ISBN 978-0-470-19588-8 (cloth)
  1. Humor in the workplace. I. Christopher, Scott, 1967– II. Title.
  HF5549.5.H85G67   2008
  658.4′5—dc22

                                                    2007051424

Printed in the United States of America.

10 9 8 7 6 5 4 3 2 1

CONTENTS

ACKNOWLEDGMENTS

This book began with a premise but was made credible with research. We owe our first and largest debt of gratitude to Amy Lyman, chair and cofounder of the Great Place to Work Institute, for her enthusiasm for this topic, the access she provided to her organization's research, and the many wonderful case studies she supplied. We also wish to thank partners, Nancy Costopoulos and Tim Keiningham, at Ipsos North America for the proprietary research they conducted on our behalf to prove these concepts.

Special thanks are due to our editors at John Wiley and Sons: Laurie Harting who had the initial vision for this work and Shannon Vargo who fleshed out the idea in vigorous form. We also wish to thank the entire Wiley marketing, sales, and publicity teams, including Kim Dayman, as well as Larry Alexander and the senior leadership group for their excitement about the project. We also wish to thank our researchers and critical readers, Glen Nelson, Christie Giles, and Jeff Birk for their valuable work. And we owe a debt to our amazing publicist Mark Fortier.

We wish to thank all of those quoted here and the many we spoke with but weren't able to include. We especially appreciate those who allowed us to watch them in action and put up with us loitering in the back of meeting rooms with clipboards in hand.

For their support and enthusiasm about this project, we thank our colleagues Chester Elton, Kent Murdock, Dave Petersen, and the rest of the Carrot Culture team. We would, of course, be remiss if we neglected to thank James Cameron and the entire production team of *Titanic,* for obvious reasons.

And finally, we wish to thank our families for their tireless love, support, and good humor during an exhausting research and writing process. To Jennifer and Tony; to Liz, Christian, Josh, Matt, Scott, and John. To them this book is dedicated.

PART I

THE CASE FOR LEVITY

Levity has an image problem.

For such a seemingly whimsical concept, it's amazing what a steaming mound of criticism it engenders in the business world. In the training we conduct with corporate groups and the coaching we perform with executives on this subject, we can't seem to get past the opening hellos before someone feverishly brings up the dark side of fun:

> "You can get too much of a good thing, you know."
>
> "People won't take their jobs seriously."
>
> "Mandatory fun is no fun at all."
>
> "My boss tries to be funny, but it's embarrassing."
>
> "I'm not humorous, and I'm never going to be."

After a few minutes of furrowed brows and increasingly volatile verbal exchanges, we arrive at the conclusion that we are either dead wrong about levity or we've accidentally been booked to speak at the annual meeting of death row clergymen.

For many, it may seem that there are a thousand reasons not to write about, read about, or even think about this subject. After all, what does levity really have to do with business? And just as we're ready to surrender our mission to scoffs, derision, and upturned schnozzes, we discover the best excuses to continue pursuing the topic: the converted.

These loyal levity believers swim upstream through the flow of conference attendees exiting after we have concluded our presentations, nodding their heads, and shaking our hands as if we're the handle on the last water pump in the Sahara. "Thank goodness you came, that was fantastic," they'll say. "My colleagues really needed to hear this message; we're so bad at this stuff."

As champions of fun at work, they are among the growing number of people who choose to lead with the Levity Effect. And thankfully for us, they aren't just a few nuts relegated to back-office jobs or Human Resources. They are usually some of the most successful, trusted, innovative people in their organizations. They are the living proof that levity is a real, positive, and valuable business practice.

And here's what they've discovered: With low unemployment rates and fierce competition for great talent, fun at work can provide a competitive advantage, help attract and retain employees, and provide the spark to jump-start creativity. Sure, it may be hard to measure the return on investment of go-cart outings, dress-up contests, or a perfectly timed punch line, but the leaders profiled in this book will attest that fun is an essential component of their people, business, and innovation strategies. In short, people tend to remain with, stay committed to, and give more energy to an organization where good times are injected into work.

Not only that, but managers who lead with levity benefit from higher levels of employee engagement and overall success. Chances are excellent that you've known a leader like this at some point in your career. Maybe you had a boss who was genuinely funny, cracking a hilarious comment now and then to loosen everyone up. Or maybe, and more likely, you had a boss who wasn't that much of a punster or a quick-quip artist, but she encouraged the group to get a little silly once in a while. In other words, she may not have been Paula Poundstone, but she was authentic, genuine, and lighthearted and she let people be themselves.

And at its core, that's what levity is about. It's not only about having fun at work, though we show you how great organizations do just that. It's not just about being humorous, though we discuss how to discover your innate wit and humor. It's not so much about being funny, it's about being fun.

CHATTERING TEETH AND A KAZOO BAND?

Perhaps you need some persuading to convince you that levity is indeed a virtue (and hopefully we won't have to resort to violence). We have plenty of real-life tales and analogies to share. Here's a quick example that happened a few years ago at the corporate offices of the world's largest restaurant chain. Like many organizations, its core values included such things as "customer focus" and "belief in people," but surprisingly, the values list also included "fun."

At the company, when someone *walked the talk,* in other words when they exemplified one or more of the corporate values, the chairman presented a Walk-the-Talk award, a novelty store set of 39-cent chattering teeth. That got our attention. It might seem like a silly prize from a chairman, but nothing could have been further from the truth. As we toured the organization's cubicle maze, we noticed the chattering teeth were everywhere, always in positions of honor. One employee had even attached dramatic lighting to the cube wall to illuminate her three sets of teeth.

The company also had what they called a "fun band," composed of bongo drummers, a host of kazooists, and even a sousaphone player. When a Walk-the-Talk award was presented, the band marched throughout the cubicle maze at corporate headquarters. It was their version of a ticker-tape parade. Several employees told us that they had unsuccessfully fought back tears of joy when first paid a visit by the chairman and the fun band.

We know you might be thinking: "Okay, they're a bit eccentric over there, but no harm done. It's not exactly *professional* behavior; I mean, that would never fly at my office."

The plot thickens.

One day, into this jolly environment came a new senior executive. The new manager first heard the boisterous band one afternoon while on a conference call with Wall Street. He was mortified. "How utterly unprofessional," he thought. He slammed his door shut and sat in his office for hours afterward, fuming.

At the next leadership meeting, the chairman asked if anyone had any other business for the quorum. The new executive cleared his throat and began. "Look," he said, "I don't know if you know this, but there's a kazoo and bongo group that marches around here. I was on the phone with an analyst last week. We're discussing a million-dollar stock purchase, and this goofy band marches by. It was embarrassing."

The room fell silent. People squirmed in their seats. Finally the chairman rose. He spoke not unkindly, but with strength. "I don't know if you've noticed our list of values posted on the walls everywhere, but one of the values is 'fun' and another is, 'walk the talk.' I guess you didn't see that I was at the head of that marching band presenting a Walk-the-Talk award in what we think is a really *fun* way. We can't pay Wall Street salaries here. We may not offer our people company cars or a lot of stock options. But we keep employees because we have fun and we live our values."

Then, the chairman added, "And if you don't get that, maybe *you* are in the wrong place."

As it turned out, the new executive was in the wrong place. About two months later, he decided to walk. He found a place without kazoos and chattering teeth. That's the thing about the Levity Effect at work: It attracts the right people and repels the wrong ones.

AND AWAY WE GO

So what is levity? In short, it means being light, buoyant even. The problem is, buoyancy doesn't sound very desirable in the business world. After all, who wants a lightweight, bouncy goof-off handling finances, piloting the plane, or dealing with upset customers? It's no wonder that fun gets a bad rap.

But levity doesn't mean silly or inane. It doesn't mean distracting. Levity is a way to improve a workplace, a presentation, or a relationship in ways that can change our work and our lives for the better.

The word itself is derived from Latin, *levitas*, the same root for the word levitate. And that's the secret to levity. It raises things. While in a business setting, some people may distrust it, but when things get tense, drab, slow, stressful, and boring, a forkfull of levity can mean the difference between working cohesively toward a goal and being hindered by contention.

Of course, we make no claims that levity will fix a toxic culture, make up for poor pay practices, improve your products, or make your workplace safe. If you lack any of those basics, read some other important leadership books first. A few suggestions include the best-selling *Some Employees Are People Too, The Importance of Paying People Actual Money Rather than Produce,* and the pretty-good-selling *Here, You Should Probably Wear this Hard Hat if You're Going to Unload that Train Car Full of Nuclear Waste.* Start there. The good news is that most of the organizations we visit have the basics down. They are simply looking for something more to give them the competitive advantage—something that provides a differentiator in today's competitive markets. They're looking for an edge.

In the following pages, we'll show you how to create that edge and how to benefit from the effects of levity.

So if you're ready, let's lighten up.

CHAPTER ONE

Levity Is a Funny Thing

If They're Busting a Gut, They'll Bust Their Butts

Two guys walk into a bar . . .

Whoa, whoa, whoa. You can't start a serious business management book with a line like that. That flies in the face of conventional wisdom. Harrumph, grumble, grumble.

Well, you can relax. This is no joke.

Two guys walk into a bar. They're both leaders at the same company. One has a big, infectious smile and is laughing as he opens the door. The guy at his side hasn't actually cracked a smile since *Laugh-In*. Quick test of your judgment skills: Which one's better at his job?

You're going to need a little more info, right? Nope. It's a simple call, and current research backs it up: The guy who's laughing and enjoying himself is

9

better. He's considerably more likely to be more productive, inspiring, engaging, committed, efficient,
secure, and trusted—overall a better leader.

Likeable sure, but why is he better?

For one thing, look at it from the point of view
of the people who work with him or for him. How
would you rather spend your days? Working with a
buttoned-down stiff whose idea of fun at work is
rolling up his sleeves or for someone who allows you
to let loose every now and then—like the employees at
Lego America who zip around campus on scooters, or
at Principal Financial Group where employees have
set up mini golf courses in their offices, or at Google
with its annual employee ski trip, or at Ben & Jerry's
where factory workers take home a couple of pints of
ice cream a week, or at *Sports Illustrated* where employees creating the "Swimsuit Edition" . . . well, we
don't know exactly what they do for fun, but we're
pretty sure it's not *buttoned-down*.

If people are having fun, they're going to work
harder, stay longer, maintain their composure in a
crisis, and take better care of the organization.

Here's one example.

An excited Kirt Womack of the Thiokol factory in
Utah sprinted into his manager's office on the first
day of spring and asked if the folks on the factory
floor could do something fun—say, head outside and
fly paper airplanes—if they met their quota two
hours early. The manager wrinkled his brow and ve-
toed the idea. Kirt persisted, "Well, then, what if we
exceed our quota by 50 percent?" Figuring he had
nothing to lose, the manager finally gave in.

Later that day, at 1:30, the manager checked on
things and found that his employees had reached

110 percent of their quota. By 3 PM, they'd sur-
passed 150 percent. The airplanes were launched,
laughter rang out, and people frolicked (funny word,
frolicked).

This tale is no big deal, right? Sure, except for
the fact that a 50 percent increase isn't exactly in-
significant. While this tale illustrates the benefits of
levity at work, it also underscores the dire need to
enlighten management. You should know what the
supervisor's initial reaction was to his workers' hitting the 150 percent production goal by 3 PM. Rather
than connecting the dots and seeing the link between the promise of fun and working harder, he instead commented, "Imagine what you guys could
have accomplished if you hadn't taken two hours off
to screw around!"

The manager's initial ignorance did little to
dissuade the workers. The kind of joyous, playful,
break-the-tension fun they engaged in is taking
place all around the world in organizations that care
about performance, retention, and profitability. Motivated purely by the opportunity to have a little fun
at work, the aviation workers increased their performance dramatically. The next week they negotiated
for a volleyball game on the factory floor as a reward
and again hit record production levels. Each week,
they continued to request fun rewards and turned in
astounding production numbers. By the third week,
when they had earned a trip offsite for ice cream
cones, the manager finally got it.

That, in a waffle cone, is the power of the Levity
Effect at work.

An increasing body of research demonstrates that
when leaders lighten up and create a fun workplace,

there is a significant increase in the level of employee trust, creativity, and communication—leading to lower turnover, higher morale, and a stronger bottom line.

The research also shows that managers who have taught themselves to be funnier are more effective communicators and better salespeople, have more engaged employees, earn a lot more than their peers, and are much thinner. Okay, maybe not the last one.

The following pages include experiences of real businesspeople we've studied across a spectrum of real industries—high tech, manufacturing, services, retail, financial services, health care, and so on. Some of these leaders didn't start out as fun-loving souls; in fact, many spent years in gray suits, brow knitting in conference rooms with their colleagues. But they all learned to shed some of their seriousness, break away from the pack of the mirthless, and carve successful, enjoyable, rewarding career paths. And a lot of their secrets to success aren't listed in the company handbook. They are the product of innovation and creativity. Few corporate manuals exist, if any, that recommend paper airplane flying in aeronautical factories or require incorporating a rap song into a memo on new commission plans. Wise leaders learn to discover for themselves the tricks of the levity trade. But, you might not believe us if we simply gave you a few examples and said, "Go. Have some fun." Instead, we'll prove to you the connection between the punch line and the bottom line through a variety of interviews with CEOs, business leaders, salespeople, ad executives, business owners, and individuals from many other walks of life. All share some similar traits, which we will explore here, and all have learned to lighten up for real, tangible results.

How they did it is what this book is all about. You'll discover how to master the Levity Effect to impact your career and your life.

THE PATH TO 'GREAT'NESS

First, the proof. Grab your spoon; here comes the pudding.

It's hard to believe that a warm and fuzzy subject such as fun could impact an organization's success. But the remarkable case for levity at work is growing, with the most convincing numbers culled from more than a decade of research by the Great Place to Work® Institute. Data from the organization's one-million-person research database reveals that "Great" companies consistently earn significantly higher marks for "fun."

Each year, the Great Place to Work® Institute asks tens of thousands of employees to rate their experience of workplace factors including, "This is a fun place to work." On *Fortune*'s "100 Best Companies to Work For" list, produced by the Great Place to Work® Institute, employees in companies that are denoted as "great" responded overwhelmingly—an average of 81 percent—that they are working in a "fun" environment. That's a compelling statistic: Employees at the best companies are also having the best time. At the "good" companies—those that apply for inclusion but do not make the top 100—only 62 employees out of 100 say they are having fun. That gap in experience is, surprisingly, one of the largest in the survey.

Now, a skeptic will ask, "Are successful companies just more fun to be in, since they are winning and profitable, or does fun create success?" It's the old, "which came first, the chicken or the egg" question. As we met with Amy Lyman, chair of the board and cofounder of the Institute, she explained that fun and success go hand in hand. And, all companies should be wondering how to have more fun.

"It's absolutely a question companies should be asking themselves because it is something that happens in great workplaces," she said. "In fact, it would be very unusual for a company to be among the '100 Best' and not score well on the fun question."

Wow. In case you didn't catch that, let us repeat it. It would be rare to be one of *Fortune*'s "100 Best Companies to Work For" and not score well on the fun question.

Correlations to fun on the 57-question survey are all "very high, very positive," Lyman added. In fact, employees who strongly agree with that statement are extremely likely—a rock solid 0.61 correlation— to also reply positively to the statement, "Taking everything into account, I would say this is a great place to work."

Lyman explained to us that as a company moves on its journey from being lousy to good to great, they must first address basic issues such as physical safety and even friendliness. But to compare, the percentage increase from the good companies up to the best on the friendliness question is just 11¼ percent. On the fun question, the gap is 29 percent.

"In other words, when companies make the leap from good to great, they must start addressing sophisticated trust issues. One corollary to developing strong bonds of trust is that people are able to also have a great deal of fun at work," Lyman says.

"If you are interested in increasing the opportunities for fun across an organization, and people genuinely engage and have fun, then that is an indication to me of a strong workplace culture that people will want to commit to. You would see a correlation between fun and reduced turnover, better recruiting, greater camaraderie . . . all those positive things you see happen in great workplaces. You can also see the exact same thing happen within a work group.

"Many people are taught that business is sterile and numbers oriented, with the human element secondary to all else," she explained. "This hard-nosed mentality goes back to a time when people were thought of as cogs in the machinery, as opposed to now, where people are seen as contributors and producers of work. Fun is part of life. When leaders see people as human beings who are more productive when they are having fun, it makes all the difference."

In fact, fun was one factor that was considered when the Great Place to Work® survey was developed. The survey statements were compiled by listening to employees' opinions on what makes an engaging workplace. As employees told their stories it was clear that the "100 Best" companies enjoyed a high level of trust. Another point that came through very clearly in employees' stories was that in the great workplaces employees were allowed to have fun on the job.

Now, organizations create fun in a hundred different ways. Intuit has a fun committee that rotates personnel every quarter and creates low-budget activities for all to participate in—everything from potluck breakfasts to Jeopardy games. AstraZeneca has a fun department that brings *funsters* to the company, singing, distributing toys, telling jokes, and doing dances to set the mood as part of their health and wellness series. Valero has volunteer bands that play at community and employee events. The list goes on and on and is detailed in later chapters.

The only rule Lyman points out is that the fun in great companies is natural, organic.

She explains, "A few years ago, one of our clients was experiencing low levels of camaraderie among employees. They decided to have an ice cream social at the end of the month with the idea that this would help with their camaraderie opportunity. As the leaders were explaining it, we realized their goal was to appease the critics. The organizers said, 'Employees complain we don't have enough fun, so we'll show them. We'll give them ice cream.'"

Through a discussion with the leaders about their intentions and the potential consequences—that employees would probably be able to see the real reason for the ice cream social—Lyman suggested that it might be more meaningful if the ice cream celebration was linked to a work achievement. The company had received a recent grant, and the employees had all contributed to this accomplishment. The lights went on for the leaders—seeing the link between fun and the celebration of an accomplishment—and the event was a lot more successful. This was a small start for this company, yet it had a big impact.

One of Lyman's favorite examples of real fun happens daily in one of the product design work groups at software giant Microsoft. As reported in their "Culture Audit" submission to the Institute, "Each day, one person signs up to blast a song across the room at three o'clock. Everyone is dragging by that point and needs a break. Some people get up and dance. Everyone claps when the song is done."

How do you create that kind of real fun? It works because there is a sense that people are all working together toward a common goal. People enjoy each other's spirit. The relationship comes before the fun, which makes the fun real and acceptable. Another company could try this, and people might get ticked off.

Lyman is quick to point out that at great companies, fun goes hand in hand with trust. "Fun benefits from high trust and vice versa," she says. "Since people are trusting, they aren't afraid to make fools of themselves and take more risks. And in turn, trust is reinforced and benefits from the fun experiences people have."

This scenario was played out at a university we studied that wanted to lighten up the dour environment. When the president asked maintenance to do something about an ugly new satellite dish on the top of a building, the crew manager gave employees the assignment and asked them to be creative in their approach. They took his request literally. Since it was fall, they painted a giant jack-o-lantern on the dish. The president and student body loved it. Now the dish is painted seasonally, and employees in the typically low-profile maintenance group can't wait for their turn to express themselves in a high-profile, fun way. That never would have happened if the employees hadn't felt enough trust in their manager to take a risk.

As will be evident in the following pages, trust gradually develops as managers show their employees that they can laugh at themselves and can use levity to diffuse tense situations. These managers come across as more approachable, which also fosters rapport and eases stressful times. They understand that levity at work doesn't just mean fun and games; sometimes it's as simple as unfurrowing a brow or relaxing clenched jaws.

No one knows this better than Jim Olson and Vern Wardle. They've worked together for decades at Harman Management Corporation, the world's first and one of the largest and most profitable Kentucky Fried Chicken franchises. Jim is the president, Vern the COO of this chain of 350 restaurants.

As background and a personal insight, Vern and his wife have long shared a secret signal: Three of anything means "I love you." It could be three honks of a horn as his wife returns home or a kitchen light flashing on and off three times before Vern leaves for an early morning flight.

One day at the office, after a heated disagreement, Vern and Jim each stormed to their adjoining offices. After a few minutes Vern was sitting at his desk, still fuming over Jim's pig-headedness, when he heard three slow, distinct knocks on the wall. He shook his head a little and grinned. Jim had used Vern's own secret message to apologize. Laughing a little to himself, Vern rapped the code back: One, two, three. "I love you, too, buddy."

Is there just a trace of a smile on your face? There were certainly grins on Jim's and Vern's faces that day. In fact, for a long time, they've been laughing all the way to the bank. That's because from a corporate perspective, managing with levity affects the bottom line. It certainly has for Harman Management and many others you'll read about.

Lyman cited a number of research studies that have linked the strong positive cultures of the "100 Best" companies with strong financial performance. If you had invested your beloved dough in the "100 Best" companies to work for over the past decade, you would have earned almost two times the return to the S&P 500 (Figure 1.1)—indicating that great workplaces produce outstanding returns for their shareholders.

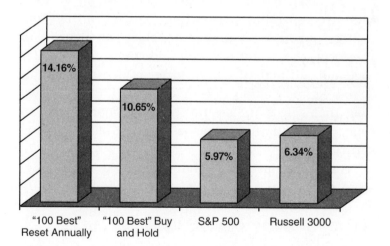

Figure 1.1   Annual Returns of *Fortune*'s "100 Best" versus the Stock Market, 1998–2006. *Source:* Russell Investment Group.

Take the example of Ann Machado, founder of Creative Staffing, an employment agency in Miami. Years ago, her company began offering fun shopping sprees by limo to her employees—and revenues grew at more than 40 percent annually. But when someone talked her into replacing the fun with traditional HR benefits, such as a new disability and pension plan, revenue growth slowed to only 9 percent annually. "We got too serious," she said. She reinstated the fun and revenues shot back up. Imagine that.

THE 'BODY' OF EVIDENCE

It turns out that fun is serious business. Still, there are a lot of seriously unfunny managers out there. And here are their names.

No, seriously. Most of the leaders we spoke with admitted spending part of their careers in the camp of the sourpuss. It's understandable. The pressure to perform, the desire to excel, and the need to justify acclaim ultimately sap leaders of their inherent, childlike inclination to seek out play and fun. They lose themselves and assume another identity that, in one form or another, squashes levity while nurturing gravity.

In a national study conducted by Harris Interactive, more than 5,700 workers were asked to identify a TV boss who reminds them of their own. Some of the most popular responses included:

- Charlie from *Charlie's Angels* (absentee)
- Judge Judy from *Judge Judy* (no nonsense)
- Donald Trump from *The Apprentice* (demanding, powerful)

- Simon Cowell from *American Idol* (judgmental, insulting)
- Mr. Burns from *The Simpsons* (sinister)
- Michael Scott from *The Office* (idiotic)
- Tyra Banks from *America's Next Top Model* (quick to point out flaws)

The results included only three positive examples:

1. Sam Malone of *Cheers* (amicable, fun)
2. Miranda Bailey from *Grey's Anatomy* (tough, but fair)
3. Jack from *Lost* (smart, looks out for the team)

In October of 2006, at our request, international research firm Ipsos conducted a 1,000-person national survey of working adults to measure the effect a manager's sense of humor has on employee retention. Survey participants were asked to rate their bosses' sense of humor, and in another part of this general consumer survey, they were asked how likely it was that they would be working for their employer a year from now. The results are illuminating:

Employee Rates Manager's Sense of Humor	Employee Rates Likelihood of Working at Current Job a Year from Now
1–6	7.75
7–10	8.96
(1–10 Scale, 10 is highest)	

The Ipsos research numbers show that employees who rated their managers' sense of humor as "above average" (a score of 7–10), rate the likelihood that they will be on the job a year from now at almost 90 percent (8.96 out of 10). But those employees who rated their managers' sense of humor as "average" or "below average," rate their chances of staying at only about 77.5 percent.

According to Tim Keiningham, senior vice president of Ipsos Loyalty, "The connection is not an anomaly. There is a statistically significant correlation between your manager's sense of humor and your willingness to remain with an organization."

Clearly, there are as many different leadership styles as there are people, but a sense of humor is essential regardless of the leadership style. In a 2007 survey by Robert Half International, of 492 employees, 65 percent said it is "very important" that managers have a sense of humor. Perhaps they understand what managers may sometimes forget: The need for fun is hardwired into our systems and has a biological impact on the body.

LAUGHTER IS THE BEST MEDICINE

In 2005, researchers at the University of Maryland School of Medicine in Baltimore showed that mental stress constricted blood vessels, reducing blood flow. Laughter, however, caused the tissue that forms the inner lining of blood vessels (the endothelium) to expand, increasing blood flow. All this science corroborates the old maxim: serious as a heart attack.

But does the magnitude of this scientific fact resonate with you? Stress reduces blood flow. Let us type this slowly so you don't read it too quickly: Stress reduces blood flow. And you know all that flowing blood? Yeah, it delivers oxygen to the brain and keeps your heart beating: two important characteristics you desire in employees.

The University of Maryland study observed 20 adults who watched clips of a violent movie (say *Pulp Fiction* or *Charlotte's Web*) and a humorous movie (like *Borat* or *Titanic*). On one hand, they found that blood flow was significantly reduced—by about 35 percent—in 14 of the subjects who watched the stressful film. On the other hand, blood flow *increased* by 22 percent in 19 of 20 volunteers after watching the funny movie. Although some *Borat* fans do seem to exhibit a certain blood flow restriction to their brains, that's another thing altogether. The research team concluded that the increased blood flow experienced by most participants was equal to that seen in individuals after 15 to 30 minutes of exercise. Tae Bo, my butt!

Dr. Lee Berk, assistant professor of family medicine at the University of Maryland and a researcher at the Susan Samuel Center for Complementary and Alternative Medicine, said, "Laughter is not dissimilar from exercise. It's not going to cure someone from stage-three cancer, but in terms of prevention, it does make sense. In a sense, we have our own apothecary on our shoulders. Positive emotions such as laughter affect your biology."

In a series of follow-up studies, Dr. Berk went on to prove that just looking forward to a humorous or lighthearted event impacts us physiologically in very positive ways. The research demonstrated that merely anticipating something funny reduces levels of at least four of the neuroendocrine hormones associated with stress. The result was a measurable change in moods: Incidence of depression fell by 51 percent, confusion went down by 36 percent, anger fell by 19 percent, fatigue by 15 percent, and tension by 9 percent.

For this reason, Hal Rosenbluth, CEO of Rosenbluth International, the nation's largest travel-services company with $2 billion in revenues, considers it "almost inhumane if companies create a climate where people can't naturally have fun." From his perspective, "Our role and responsibility as leaders and associates is to create a place where people can enjoy themselves. I know our company is doing well when I walk around and hear people laughing. The enjoyment translates into performance."

Art Hargate, CEO of Ross Environmental Services, a heavily regulated company in a highly policed industry (hazardous waste), told us that his firm has a long-standing tradition of being serious. "We're in a very serious business, and the margin of error is very narrow. The regulatory environment is very strict, and there are nasty penalties . . . our customers expect us to be very serious people about what we do. Our work environment is very serious, very intense. So lightening up is hard for us. Over the years, I've always thought, 'Geez, the pressure is so intense, maybe it's bad for people. The constant stress response is one that I feel like over time can be debilitating. We've got to lighten up."

Since they started lightening up a few years ago, the company has experienced record growth each year. Coincidence? Hardly. Hargate says, "I think lightening up a bit has helped our productivity and made it easier for us to grow. It actually improves our focus and quality of output."

HUMOR IS A FUNNY THING

Of course, all of this begs the question: Why doesn't every leader incorporate more levity into their interactions with employees? Simply put, they don't know how.

Remember the day you were first promoted to a position of leadership? (Congratulations, by the way.) Suddenly, you were in charge of leading a new group of people. This was *your* crew. You were the captain. The ship sailed under your command and, by golly, you would sail the hell out of it. Ahhhrggh, ya scallywag.

In the excitement to don your tassel-shouldered uniform and Cap'n Crunch hat, in your rush to hoist the main mast and grasp the wheel, setting course for the wide open seas of corporate success, in your eager attempt to bark out your first orders to "heave" and "look lively," you suddenly realize that you have absolutely no idea how to actually lead the crew to do (Cap'n) Jack Squat.

You don't really know how to connect with your people as a leader because up until now you've never needed to. That was always someone else's burden. You just played your role. Maybe your promotion to management was more the result of doing your job well or bringing some new-fangled idea to the table rather than your ability to manage a team of actual human beings. Perhaps your recent work significantly contributed to the bottom line. You made the bosses a little richer, so, wham! Here's your reward: a nice, new title along with some added responsibilities.

Let's stay with the pirate ship analogy—if for no other reason than to torture you. Maybe you moved up through the ranks. You started as a mere swabbie. Did that for nigh on ten year. Somebody stabbed the First Mate between the shoulder blades (probably you), and you took the post. Now, after more'n two-score year of sailin', you've moved up to Cap'n, cuz you outlived the rest . . . and you've got a killer eye patch and teeth composed of various precious metals.

Of course, we can't ignore the possibility that you just flat-out deserve this position. (But where's the fun in that?) You did the education thing, got your MBA, have read all the best-selling business books and attended dozens of continuing education courses and seminars. You wear power attire and can recite the *Seven Habits* in your sleep, backwards, and in Mandarin, *nee pow*. But most important, you know the business.

However you got here, you are now responsible for managing other people, getting them to *do stuff,* and as great as you were in your old position, it doesn't mean much if you can't lead people out of a soaking wet paper bag. General George S. Patton said, "Leadership is the art of getting someone else to do something you want done because he wants to do it."

So why is levity the answer?

For one, studies on group decision making show that people who use more humor tend to yield greater influence over group decisions. People just work

harder for people they like. We reject that old Machi-
avellian garbage about, "It's better to be feared than
loved, if you cannot have both." We're pretty sure
Machiavelli just sat around in his prince suit thinking up memorable quotes on leadership rather than
actually leading anybody anywhere. Today's equivalent rhetoric would be, "I don't care if they hate me,
as long as they respect me!" Pretty sensible philosophy (snort).

Imagine this scenario: Milton and Lois are sip-
ping their morning coffee as they walk down the cor-
ridor at Frigsten Incorporated.

Milton: Ugh! I can't stand our boss. The very thought
of him turns my stomach.
Lois: (agreeing) Absolutely hate his guts.
Milton: Seriously, I just flat-out despise his existence.
Lois: You got that right. If he were to die tomorrow in
a grisly gardening accident, I wouldn't even shed
a tear.
Milton: The man is a blight. An embarrassment to
human reproduction.
Lois: Hate. His. Guts.
Milton: Ditto. But you gotta respect him.
Lois: Oh yeah, no doubt. Totally respect him. Tons
of respect.
Milton: Me too, hands down. But I still hate him.
Lois: Can't even breathe for the hatred!

Levity helps foster respect and positive relationships with employees. It also makes the work itself
more palatable. Consider how much your employees
would begrudge the assignment of walking around
for hours in 100-degree heat or in the pouring rain.

Yet, put some on a golf course, and they would do it gladly. (Some would even pay for the privilege.) The difference between the two scenarios is the addition of fun (though we personally wonder how much fun it is to break a three iron over your knee while using curse words that would embarrass Sarah Silverman).

Incorporating levity into your leadership style makes sense on so many levels, yet many of us still would rather walk the plank (sorry knave, that's the end of the pirate lingo) than attempt it. It's the unfortunate result of a common misconception.

For some reason, many of us have arrived at the conclusion that if somebody has a good sense of humor, it means they're funny. The truth is that humor doesn't always evoke laughter. Researchers Lawrence J. Peter and Bill Dana say, "A sense of humor is deeper than laughter, more satisfying than comedy, and delivers more rewards than merely being entertaining. A sense of humor sees the fun in everyday experiences. It is more important to have fun than it is to be funny."

It's also a heck of a lot easier, especially if your idea of killer material is something you found on a Bazooka bubble gum wrapper. Let's face it; if you only think a sense of humor is to make others laugh, you're in for some serious blows to your self-esteem. At one time or another, we've all put on an awkward grin while a coworker tried to be funny and ended up being pathetic, or worse, offensive.

If you can somehow develop a true *sense* of humor and not worry about just being funny, you'll achieve much more than managers who force comedy on an unwilling/unsuspecting audience.

Have you ever heard of Ty Brown? Probably not. He's not a movie star. He's not a politician. He's not a world-class athlete, or even village-class for that matter. But Ty Brown has something that all of us who take levity seriously should strive for: a top-notch laugh.

His office is just twenty feet or so from ours, and we frequently get to hear his robust laugh. It's truly inspiring. It has to be one of the best, jovial, authentic laughs on the planet today. It's never forced or fake. Ty's not an obnoxious, frequent laugher. It only happens when it's supposed to, and boy is it worth the wait. It puts a smile on our faces. It wakes us up. Doesn't matter what we're doing—dealing with a demanding client, sorting out travel plans, or working out the kinks in a new product—one blast of that laugh brings smiles to the faces of all colleagues within earshot, as well as some needed perspective to the grind.

A person with a laugh like that could ask you to empty the contents of your purse or wallet into his hands "for the good of the company" and you'd do it. Look up "infectious" in the dictionary and you'll find a photo of Ty Brown laughing . . . and one of a leper colony.

Leading with levity is the willingness to laugh and find humor even in the most difficult situations. Abraham Lincoln once interrupted a meeting to read an amusing story in the hopes of dispelling a black cloud that was hovering over his staff. With the tragic Civil War unfolding before their eyes, no one so much as smiled at the president's attempt at humor. Finally, Lincoln stiffened and said, "Gentlemen, why don't you laugh? With the fearful strain that is upon me day and night, if I did not laugh, I should die, and you need this medicine as much as I do."

Aside from a desire to make others laugh, it's important to take time out for fun activities. "Whenever we have a board of directors meeting, we always create some kind of activity along with it," said Jim Olson, president of Harman Management. "So maybe our meeting goes until 2 PM, and we're over in Hawaii, so we take a break, put everyone on a bus, take 'em over to Tommy Bahamas to get 'em all swimsuits and T-shirts, and then come back to the hotel, and go play volleyball. It's the intangible of having something fun to do and the playfulness that comes out in that process that I believe helps us work better not just as business associates, but also as people and friends. It's kind of a leveler. When somebody is dominant in the boardroom, and you get out on the volleyball court and someone else is dominant, you realize people contribute in different ways."

None of the core principles of levity leadership involves repeating verbatim every sophomorically hilarious line from *Dumb and Dumber* in your next production meeting, though that level of levity may have its place from time to time. But that kind of commitment to levity takes a lot of time, effort, and a photographic memory, at a minimum. The ideal methods are much easier than that. As Olson exemplifies, leading with levity is about a lightness of manner and a willingness to enjoy the moment. It's a smile on your face and in your voice. It's an attitude of latitude. It's allowing levity to happen.

Being funny is one thing. Being fun is everything. Stand-up comedy is a skill only a few people

can master; leading with levity is som
willing leader of people can learn.

ALTRUISM ASIDE, WHAT'S IN IT FOR ME?

There is little doubt that many truly effective leaders
understand and wisely wield the power of levity, and
with good reason. For each levity action we include
in our daily routine, there is a resulting effect. In the
following chapters, we will address each levity action
and its levity effect:

Levity Action		Levity Effect
Humor	→	Communication
Fun	→	Creativity
Respect	→	Trust
Lightness	→	Health
Wit	→	Wealth

Of all the reasons to incorporate levity into the
workday, the most seductive by far for most of us is
the last. The *Harvard Business Review* reports that
executives with a sense of humor climb the corporate
ladder more quickly and actually earn more money
than their peers. Why? Quite simply, executives hire
and promote the humorous more often than the
dour. Wouldn't you?

A Hodge-Cronin & Associates survey of 737 chief
executives of major corporations showed that an
amazing 98 percent said they would hire a person
with a good sense of humor over one who seemed to
lack a sense of levity. That's just about unanimous.

This survey may appear rather pedestrian until you consider that chief executives typically only get involved in hiring decisions for the very top levels of management and leadership. And when they do, they're looking for someone who can communicate, who can inspire others to follow, who can, in short, lead with levity.

It was just such a CEO who hired us years ago and trusted us to start a new business line in an 80-year-old company. In two years, using the principles of the Levity Effect, we built a multimillion-dollar speaking and training business from nothing, within a very traditional company that had never done anything like it before.

Still, there were plenty of brow knitters along the way, those skeptics who wanted to tell us what to do, and mostly, what not to do. We had executives argue that we should make our training offering more dignified and less fun. And we were almost convinced. That is, until a visit with a major client assured us we were on the right track.

A vice president of The Pepsi Bottling Group put it this way, "I can get similar content from other training companies, but I can't get the humor you offer. I want my people to love this training or they won't pay attention."

So we went back and made our training even funnier, and more people hired us.

When we took our team speed golfing or broke for afternoon foosball tournaments or Frisbee tosses, the corporate types frowned. When we stopped work at stressful times to throw multicolored plastic balls back and forth across the cubicle plains, we were reported to HR. When we had a crazy ceremony to present awards for such things as the "most offensive remark" made to a trainer or the "most miles flown in coach hell," the accounting department questioned the expenses.

Our CEO just smiled.

And with that ally, we held our ground. We took our team from nothing to millions in revenue with a handful of employees. We saw the brand evolve and increased our numbers of clients exponentially along the way. Now, the company uses the enterprise as a hood ornament for everything it is doing.

Our small success cut against the grain of conventional business thinking, yet we continue to grow because we understand the power of levity at work. Our growth is not the result of badgering, threats, and harrumphing but of laughter and creativity.

Funny, isn't it? In the current business climate, where half of all employees report having experienced verbal abuse and yelling and most businesses are spending enormous amounts of time and money searching for a competitive advantage, the solution may be as simple as just learning how to lighten up.

Let's see how.

SIDELIGHT
THE LEVITY LITMUS TEST

11 QUESTIONS TO CHECK YOUR
ENVIRONMENT'S FUN pH

Most companies profess to have fun. It has even become more common for some corporate mission statements to mention fun as a value held near and dear to the company. But few organizations really walk the talk.

When you think about your organization or when you consider joining a new company, ask yourself the following questions to gauge the levity quotient of your boss, team, and culture. A score of 40 or higher means there's a good chance you'll enjoy working there for the long term.

You've done this before: One means never, two is hardly, three is neutral, four is most of the time, and five is just about always. Circle the number and keep score:

New employees are made to feel welcome.	1 2 3 4 5
Meetings are positive and light.	1 2 3 4 5
We have fun activities at least once a month.	1 2 3 4 5
It's common to hear people laughing around here.	1 2 3 4 5
I can be myself at work.	1 2 3 4 5
We have a lot of celebrations for special events.	1 2 3 4 5
When brainstorming, we like to have fun.	1 2 3 4 5
My boss is usually optimistic and smiling.	1 2 3 4 5
Customers would call us fun to do business with.	1 2 3 4 5
I have a friend at work who makes me laugh.	1 2 3 4 5
We have a good time together.	1 2 3 4 5

40 or above: Congratulations. Your work environment ranks among the best. Geez, maybe *you* should have written this book.

30–40: You need to lighten up to enhance employee engagement, creativity, and loyalty.

30 or below: You have terminal seriousness. Call us.

CHAPTER TWO

Levity Effect— Communication

If They're Laughing, They're Listening

Who hasn't suffered through a business meeting so dull, so mind-numbingly dreadful that even the presenter seemed ready to nod off? Or witnessed keynote speakers who could moonlight as hypnotists, what with all the glazed eyes in the audience? Why put us through that torture? And what did we take away from the bore-a-thon besides a desire to step in front of a charging water buffalo? Probably not much.

Whether you're about to make a presentation to senior management to get funding for your big idea (outsourcing to primates), to pitch a sale to a prospect who could make your year, or trying to engage a troop of distracted Camp Fire Girls, great communicators know that a little humor goes a long

way toward making you and your messages more
memorable.

Consider the use of humor in advertising. While
statistics, sales, and sex are still used to great effect
in certain ads, the proliferation of humor in media
over the last few decades can't be ignored. Beer companies, ironically, whose traditional aim is to glam-
orize and romance their products, have shifted their
objective from titillation to tickling funny bones.
Think of all the millions of dollars spent on Super
Bowl ads in just 2007 alone, and those you're likely
to remember made you laugh (see Table 2.1).

Linda Kaplan Thaler, CEO of one of the nation's
fastest-growing advertising agencies and author of
the best seller *The Power of Nice*, says humor is increasingly used in advertising because it is usually
the most effective way to move business forward. In
fact, she is famous for using humor to stand out in
traditionally buttoned-down categories.

Years ago, her organization was pitching the
Aflac account in the very serious insurance business. "They had traditionally been using very heart-
felt, mushy-like-a-warm-cookie advertising," she told
us. Kaplan Thaler realized Aflac's biggest problem
was not a lack of differentiation in their market, but
the simple fact that no one could remember the
name. In fact, even her creative people kept asking
her to repeat the name of company again. "Aflac,
Aflac," was heard over and over in the halls.

She recalls, "Finally an art director put his fingers over the nose of the writer and said, 'Say that
again. You know, you sound like a duck quacking.'"

Kaplan Thaler had the good sense to think the
idea had merit and suggested taking it to the client.

Table 2.1 10 Highest-Rated 2007 Super Bowl Ads

Product	Description	Score
Bud Light	Owners demonstrate how their dogs fetch Bud Light.	9.04
Pepsi	Bears find food and an empty Pepsi cooler in a cabin.	8.88
Budweiser	Donkey dreams of being a Clydesdale.	8.83
Bud Light	A romantic sleigh ride goes amiss.	8.62
Frito-Lay	Grandma and Grandpa fight over a bag of Lay's.	8.50
7Up	Rolling slam-dunk contest.	8.45
Bud Light	Dale Earnhardt Jr. returns lipstick.	8.34
Budweiser	Referee tunes out coach angry over call.	8.18
Bud Light	Cedric gets an unexpected spa treatment.	8.07
Nextel	Dale Earnhardt Jr. scores touchdown in racer.	7.89

Source: USA Today.

And the rest is history, right? Not quite. The client hated it. In fact, she recollects them saying, "Are you kidding? A duck is going to be our insurance salesman?" Aflac was so skeptical they wouldn't even spring for a market test of the commercial, so Kaplan Thaler paid for a TV test from her own pocket. "And it tested through the roof. We won the business. Now when people see ducks they immediately think of supplemental insurance at work," she jokes.

Indeed, humor such as Aflac's works on TV. But humor also works in the classroom. In fact, college students are more likely to recall a lecture when it is sprinkled with jokes. Sam Houston State University psychologist Randy Gardner's fascinating research showed that when levity about relevant topics was injected into lectures, students scored an amazing 15 percent higher on exams than their nonhumored, bored-to-drooling peers. That's the difference between an A and a B– . . . or maybe between pass and fail.

Some leaders worry, however, that humor dilutes the message, makes it less urgent, and torpedoes credibility. Nothing could be further from the truth. Sending a message with levity demonstrates a clear understanding of the principles of effective communication. It also shows the audience that you value their time enough to want to entertain and connect with them and make it worth their while.

Take, for example, the 2007 Boston Pizza Franchise Conference.

Every two years, Canada's largest casual dining restaurant chain brings together all the franchisees from throughout North America and Mexico. You know the kind of corporate event we're talking about: a three-day-long business blowout and lunch buffet extravaganza. PowerPoints start to blur by the afternoon of the first day, and you have a hard time remembering whether the last person speaking was a man, woman, or Euphegenia Doubtfire.

But Boston Pizza executives believe in levity, so things at their meetings are a little different. At the 2007 meeting, for instance, the executive team had to introduce a new menu and store design. But rather than asking the head of marketing to give an informative yet totally forgettable speech . . . well, here's what happened:

At the appointed time, the room went dark and a video began playing on the screen. Here was a movie showing a deserted highway, and broken down on the side of the road were president, Mark Pacinda, executive vice president of corporate services, Al Cave, and vice president of marketing, Joanne Forrester. The three stood forlornly next to their car in the middle of the road. The hood was raised, and steam billowed out of the radiator. The trio wondered what to do next when Pacinda mentioned seeing a building down the road. They began to trudge toward the dilapidated structure, which housed a gas station and restaurant.

As they entered the eatery in the film, a curtain was drawn back, and the three executives walked into a stage set of a restaurant that had been built in the conference room. They were greeted by a sharp-tongued waitress and a surly restaurant owner—professional actors who had been hired to up the entertainment ante.

It quickly became evident that the restaurant was poorly run, with no menu, and horrible guest service. But because they were stranded waiting for the tow truck, Forrester suggested, "Look, while we're here, why don't we share some ideas on what we're planning on doing with our menu next year."

Over the next hour, they presented the new menus and store designs, and it was one of the most outstanding presentations we've seen in any corporate setting. Not only was the presentation very, very funny, but also their main points were impossible to forget. They knew that if they got the audience laughing, the attendees wouldn't want to miss a second of it.

Now, none of these three executives were seasoned performers. Far from it. They were a little stiff, worried about their lines now and then, and were harassed repeatedly by the two professional actors playing the owner and server. Their well-practiced one-liners were so awkward they were hilarious. The audience was laughing so hard that most still had tears in their eyes as they streamed out of the presentation.

We were asked to speak the next day of the conference, and the group was still buzzing about the skit. Most of the franchisees said it was the most memorable exchange of information they had ever been a part of, and they were thrilled that their executive team could laugh at themselves. The group of normally reserved leaders had won the audience over by incorporating fun, and they got their message across in spades.

That's not the only example at this firm but a part of Boston Pizza's strategy of incorporating levity into every aspect of their business—from the kitchen to the serving floor, from head office to training. And is it working? A resounding, "Oh sure, you betcha." Not only has Boston Pizza grown to be the number-one casual dining restaurant in Canada with more than $650 million in sales annually, but it has achieved platinum status as one of the 50 best managed companies in Canada as named by the *National Post,* Queens School of Business, and Deloitte & Touche. High praise indeed. Pass the breadsticks.

THE THESIS AND ANTITHESIS
OF LAUGHTER

In the second part of this book, we get into the nitty-gritty strategies of *how* you can lighten up to great effect in your verbal and written communication. In this chapter, we show *why* levity is vital in communication through some great examples of business leaders who incorporate humor into their work lives. Their wisdom shows how all of us can lighten up and create what we call MIRTH:

More Efficient Meetings

Informal Relationships with Employees

Remarkable Presentations

Training That Sizzles

Humorous Communication

Now, to back up a bit, while some great communicators instinctively understand the power of mirth and come by humor easily, many of us have to get there through the school of hard knocks or at very least the academy of pummeling. Memorable levity just doesn't come naturally for most people, and most leaders we start working with fall into one of the two following camps:

JAW CLENCHERS AND
BROW KNITTERS

The *jaw clencher* is indigenous to all industries, fields, professions, and disciplines. Undoubtedly one inhabits your work environment. A jaw clencher is easily identified by a mouth clamped tightly shut to allow for teeth grinding and/or lip pursing. The nostrils flare to facilitate labored, audible nasal breathing. Most also display prominent, pulsating rear jawbones (not unlike fish gills) caused by the pressure of grinding molars.

Jaw clenchers not only possess Death Valley–dry communication styles, but are also characterized by their hell-bent determination to suck any conceivable particle of joy from themselves and everyone around them for the "good of the organization." They are the human equivalent of a desiccant pack. If they were to vocalize their leadership philosophy, it would sound something like, "This is *war*, people!" or "If we don't do this right, some of us will be killed!" and "Wipe that grin off your face, happy boy, this ain't no laughing matter." Jaw clenchers do not smile, grin, wink, or "blow things off." They are riveted by the deadly seriousness of their mission, and you'd better be too, or else.

In contrast, the equally toxic *brow knitter* is mostly docile in her seriousness. Smiles or other expressions of levity only surface when a brow knitter sorts out a problem mentally, and thus, finds a degree of self-satisfaction. If coworkers or subordinates display playfulness, it is met by strained patience or indifference from the brow knitter who may exhibit a quizzical, knitted brow, as if wondering, "What could any of this jocularity have to do with saving the world, which is what we do here at Acme Rivet and Bolt?"

You may recognize some brow-knitter or jaw-clencher characteristics in yourself, and that's normal. Well, actually . . . no, it's not. It's common but not normal. But the good news is you can evolve and assimilate. In fact, it's imperative that you do if you want to have people follow you, buy from you, or listen to you. Research increasingly shows that a sense of humor is essential for great communication. Humor is shown to:

- Enhance negotiation skills
- Build rapport between leaders and employees
- Grab attention
- Relax listeners, making them more receptive to your message
- Make the information more memorable

As a businessperson, your ability to communicate is paramount to your success. A recent study revealed that the most significant work-related employee complaint was poor communication with management; and an amazing 64 percent of employees claimed that poor communication interfered with their work.

MORE EFFICIENT MEETINGS

You can think of levity as the grease in the machine of any business gathering; it smoothes interactions, moving decisions along. A fascinating, but totally boring, study examined hours of videotaped meetings conducted by six management groups. During the periods when the researchers were not lulled into a coma by the videos, they observed that each of the meetings opened with a complaining and sometimes adversarial tone. Humor was infrequent. When it was employed at all, it was largely sarcasm used to express discontent with alternative points of view, emphasizing the differences between people at the meeting. As a result, only one or two participants laughed at the remarks, and the ridicule tended to further divide the group. Little progress was made toward consensual solutions until the pattern of joking changed to a more open, inclusive style, which drew laughs from the whole group.

Researchers reported that the humor was found to, "facilitate a transition from a feeling of tension and defensiveness to a realization of relative safety and playfulness. This shared comic vision seemed to create a working bond overcoming previous estrangement . . . it cultivated a climate in which creative, playful, unconventional problem solving could mature." See, it's the lube in the engine (we recommend three quarts of 10W-40).

Following this cognitive shift, the groups on the videos progressed much more rapidly through the decision-making process. Why? Because humor forces us to look at a situation from different perspectives, enabling us to examine a broader set of alternatives.

Amy Lyman, chair of the Great Place to Work® Institute, has hundreds of examples from her research demonstrating this to be true in the best organizations. "Fun at work is part of that continuum of getting to cooperation and commitment and helping people to work well together. When people are able to have a diversion from work it gives their brains a chance to process things in ways they might not normally think about so they can go back to their task with a renewed energy or new perspective."

In our work, while writing articles or preparing presentations, we will lock ourselves in what we call the "war room," spending hours pounding on keyboards and tossing around ideas. When the ideas cease flowing, we'll stop and talk about last night's episode of *The Biggest Loser* or leave the room and play foosball for 15 minutes. We return to our work with our minds reset and with fresh perspectives on the tasks at hand.

Victor Angelo is executive representative of the U.N. Secretary-General in war-ravaged Sierra Leone. In this delicate diplomatic position, he says he frequently uses fun in meetings to not only recharge energy, but to break down deeply ingrained racial and social-class barriers.

Several times each year, he takes employees away from the capital for a two-night retreat. "We discuss business, but we also have all kinds of games, things that are simple that can have no misunderstanding. We work in a very diverse cultural environment and you have to pay attention to those sensitivities. We have colleagues who are Christians, Muslims, and some are very traditional. So you have to do things they feel comfortable with. Whatever game takes place, they need to be able to talk to their families about it. We organize three-legged races, funny soccer games . . . that create an atmosphere that brings people together and overcomes their inhibitions. The games are about bringing the walls down."

Ann Norman, one of Victor's U.N. colleagues, told us, "I've never laughed so hard in my life than during Victor's retreats. But after the laughter, he always taught a valuable lesson."

And the laughter and lessons work. Said Angelo, "When I came to Sierra Leone, there was a very big divide between some of the nationals in the office who had their roots in the city—they were considered the

elites—and those who had roots in the countryside—
they were considered the indigenous. The elite were
the descendants of former slaves who had come from
America or Europe, and they looked at their colleagues as guys from the bush. From these games and
retreats in a relaxed, nontraditional environment, we
managed to bring down these very serious barriers
and discrimination. It had been affecting even job allocation; the best jobs were going to people in their
group. That's no longer the case. Now, people are seen
first as colleagues and secondly on what they can deliver, not on their social or geographic origins."

Improved decision making in meetings, breaking
down barriers—laughter is serious business that
doesn't feel that way at all. Just ask Nina McVey, assistant vice president of human resources at Enterprise Rent-A-Car, about the "Happy Dance."

"I have a couple people on my team that when
things really do get intense they do a thing called
the 'Happy Dance.' It's a little hard to describe, and
frankly, it's not something we do in the middle of
the hallway in front of everyone, but for us it's
about taking a moment to relax, laugh a little, and
then refocus."

Whenever the group realizes they're stuck and
not getting anywhere fast, they take a moment to
laugh together, and then they get back in and solve
the problem together with a new perspective. Now
that's sound business sense.

INFORMAL RELATIONSHIPS
WITH EMPLOYEES

The "Switcheroo" sounded like a comical experiment
to Boston Pizza International CEO Mike Cordoba and

a way to engage the organization humorously, but it became something more. While being filmed by a national television network in Canada, he swapped places with a server for three days.

"He traded in his BlackBerry, his Mercedes, and his personal trainer," said Caroline Schein, vice president, People Development at Boston Pizza. "He got a booklet of bus tickets, a car that broke down, and [he] had to work split shifts with no time left for the gym. He was working in the kitchen and serving. He was a fish out of water, wondering, 'How do I make pizza dough?' So it was pretty funny."

But while thousands of viewers were laughing, Cordoba was listening and learning from his employees.

Schein added, "Mike had a great time, but he also compiled a huge list of to-do items. We needed a better kids' program and better charts for new employees who are coming in and learning products—like how to make a pizza. Our kitchen appliances needed to be more user-friendly. And so on."

Employees were learning too—that their leader was seeing what challenges they faced every day and that he didn't take himself too seriously. That's important, because levity creates an emotional bond between employees and their leaders.

"When a group or team is having fun together, there is a sense of belonging," said Schein. "You are in on the jokes, you feel in with the team. When a team is jelling like that, well, then anything is possible. In every team I've ever worked on, I've seen levity create more productivity."

A recent study by Penn State University came to the same conclusion. It found that managers who produced the highest levels of employee and organizational performance use humor the most often.

"In order to create a fun work environment, the leader must lead by example," said Schein. "They must be willing to be a little goofy and have fun. We really stress the importance of 'fun' and 'You're Among Friends' [Boston Pizza's internal and external tag line], and we emphasize what it means to have fun among friends. We want customers to come in and have a great time, and we want our employees to have a great time at work."

Says Julie Cookson, senior vice president of Scripps Networks, owner of The Food Network, HGTV, and other successful cable channels, "We try to inject humor where appropriate; it makes our executives approachable to employees. It also makes them human and demonstrates that they can balance work demands with a sense of humor," she said. "Our networks are 24/7, we are constantly looking at merger and acquisition opportunities, and we are creating high-visibility brands and sustaining them. So we are serious when we have to be, but employees know our management can have fun too."

In fact, Scripps Networks has eight core values. Among shared responsibility, integrity, diversity, and so on is the value of "humor."

With humor as a core value, the 1,400 employees know that they have a sanctioned pressure release valve to be human and let their hair down once in a while. And the executive team leads the way, known for their karaoke singing, a CFO who dons various costumes at company meetings, or dressing up as "Management in Black" and singing a parody of the movie's song. Most recently, employees and executives alike enjoyed a lighthearted race on tricycle-like "Green Machines" as part of the company's United Way fund-raising drive.

Said Cookson, "We spend more time with our coworkers than we do with our families, and I know all companies are struggling with this. If you can't find ways to balance things out and still have fun, you are going to have problems. To connect with and retain your employees, you first have to let them know you value them, and enjoying a good laugh is one of the best ways to make that connection."

Tim Fernandez, general manager of the Yamaha Marine Division Outboard Group in Atlanta, thinks one of the most important things to encourage productivity with his employees doesn't have much to do with work at the office at all.

"Like many places we have an after-hours softball team. But that only reaches a dozen or so people. But we invite everyone to come and cheer the team on; and, to include those who can't make it, I write a news column after the games. I write it like an Associated Press article, but in a funny light. I wondered if people were really reading them, but then I was late sending one, and I had a bunch of people mad at me."

Here's a brief excerpt from one of Tim's stories:

When the game came to a close the scoreboard lit up to show **CRITTER CATCHERS 7, TEAM YAMAHA 9.** It had appeared as though Team Yamaha had defeated the championship-caliber Critter Catchers, but on closer inspection it was painfully apparent that the scoreboard had been experiencing light problems and was unable to display the 2 that preceded the 7 on the Catchers side of the scoreboard. Sadly for Team Yamaha, the number 9 stood alone.

Coach Fernandez had this to say about Team Yamaha and their fans. "We may have lost the game tonight, but we were not outplayed. We hustled and we never gave up. As long as our fans continue to come to see us play, we will give them a show. Our fans are second to none."

Besides softball, the Yamaha employees in the Outboard Group find a plethora of other sporting and competitive activities to get involved in with the encouragement and participation of their boss. "There's a running joke around here that I'm not just the General Manager, I'm the Game Master," said Fernandez. "And that's okay. We have fun if the work gets done, and it always does. In a lot of offices, people are waiting for five o'clock to come around so they can run out the door. In this office, people aren't watching the clock. They work till the work gets done. They are working hard, having fun, and getting results."

Creating those informal moments is the trick. Carlos Alicea, a manager/owner of a Kentucky Fried Chicken restaurant in northern California, told us he holds a barbecue for his employees on the last Friday of each month. He knows how important it is for his employees to get out of the restaurant, socialize with each other, and build friendships. He says he barbecues, "anything but chicken," because what fun would that be? Meanwhile his restaurant enjoys some of the lowest employee turnover in the chain—are you ready?— under 100 percent! (Typical is 200–300 percent.) They love their boss and the fact that he can lighten up a bit by feeding them "anything that 'mooed' or 'oinked.'"

REMARKABLE PRESENTATIONS

George Bernard Shaw said, "If you're going to tell people the truth, you'd better make them laugh. Otherwise, they'll kill you."

Or, at the very least, ignore you, says Linda Kaplan Thaler, CEO of the billion-dollar Kaplan Thaler Group. You know her creative work if you've ever sung along to "I don't want to grow up, I'm a Toys R Us kid," or laughed when Julia Louis-Dreyfus colored a woman's hair with Nice 'n Easy on a bus.

But while Kaplan Thaler is famous for using humor to stand out in traditionally conservative categories—such as insurance and women's cosmetics to name just two—she wouldn't have had a chance to create those memorable campaigns if she hadn't won the business in the first place. And, she says, those wins are often due to the humor her team uses in presentations.

"I'm always trying to lighten it up," she said. "We were pitching an account for Panasonic. Our strategy was that no one likes to shave, which was the understatement of the year. In fact, 15 agencies were pitching the account and all were going to end up doing the same pitch. So we needed to find a way to be more creative and funny. So I wrote a song called 'Shaving Sucks.'"

As the business meeting began, Kaplan Thaler and her team sat around a conference table with the executives from this electronics giant. The Panasonic brass was expecting a formal presentation, but instead Kaplan Thaler smiled and said, "Pretend I'm one of the guys." Then she proceeded to sing, "Shaving sucks, shaving sucks, like a Band-Aid getting stuck, why does half the human race tear the hair out of their face . . ."

After sitting through days of drab pitches, the executives were very quickly snorting and hooting in appreciation of the zany song.

"They loved it, and we got the business. They said you didn't have the best strategy, but you had the most entertaining way to do it. So we figured you guys are going to be a lot of fun and more entertaining to work with."

She concludes: "There's a silent, secret rule that no one really shares (in advertising). Very often the agency that most entertains the client wins the business."

The importance of humor in presentations was a lesson learned long ago by Victor Angelo of the United Nations. With the people of Sierra Leone, many of whom had came from situations where they had a very close connection with nature, he uses humorous fables in his presentations to make strong points to employees in a nonthreatening, humorous way.

"Early [in my time] here [at Sierra Leone], I told the group a story of two mules. One was very lazy and one very hard working. The owner was carrying goods on the two mules from one part of the country to another part. The lazy one would not take a big load, so in the evening, the owner would give more food to the mule that would do more work. The lazy mule would complain. Eventually, after listening to the complaints for too long, the owner came to the conclusion that one mule could do all the work and he gave the other away. But no one wanted a lazy mule, so the only thing he could do was sell the hide. Because I added a lot of detail, humor, and relish, the employees were all laughing by the end of the story. They were also a little shocked by the message, but they could relate to the story and were eager to discuss it.

"It's not childish. We all like to learn with stories. And they think about their own circumstances and situation. How they work and how they relate to each other."

Even telling a joke outright can make a point, without being offensive. Consider just one:

"A managed care administrator dies and goes to Heaven. She can't believe her good fortune in being there, given the life she's led in rejecting so many medical claims. But St. Peter checks the records and says, 'There's no mistake. You're supposed to be here. See, it says right here that you are scheduled for Heaven. You are authorized for three days.'"

Get the point? We guarantee others will get it, too, when you address sticky subjects with humor.

Simply telling someone in a business presentation, "This is what I want you to do and how I want it done," is no guarantee that they'll actually do it or even that they are listening to you at all.

"If all you do is come to work, and you are just business, business, business, people don't necessarily listen to you," said Yamaha's Fernandez. "They lose interest. People want to be entertained. Even at work."

You might be annoyed by that statement at first. After all, you're not running a comedy cabaret; you're running a Cinnabon, or whatever. You are paying your employees, your clients need your products, your patients need to listen to your advice, your students won't graduate if they don't learn from you, and so on. But consider this: Most people speak at an average rate of 150 words per minute, but the average listener can take in anywhere from 350 to 600 words per minute. See the problem? We are biologically programmed to zone out. Research shows that the average adult has an attention span of six minutes. So that three-hour safety training session you're planning had better be packed with gory accident videos or something funny or you're in serious danger of an apathetic audience, at best. Sad, but true.

That's why many leaders follow the Zap Rule, which is basically this: Audiences need a zap at least once every three to six minutes during a presentation to stay focused and interested.

"I'm always on my toes," says Fernandez. "If you are paying attention in meetings, you will think of funny things. And those comments get people to focus. But if you are drifting off in another world, you won't spot the opportunities for humor."

For example, in a sales meeting Fernandez will often tease his customers and get them laughing. He's even been known to bring a digital camera to a convention and snap pictures of people he knows who will enjoy a joke. Then he'll spend the evening in his hotel room finding celebrity photos online that match up with the customers and employees whose pictures he's taken. Often he'll find remarkable similarities, right down to the clothes or hand gestures and poses. The next day he uses separated-at-birth slides every few minutes throughout his presentations to keep the audience rapt. Nobody dares doze off or send text messages for fear of missing out on the laugh. At a recent event, a photo of John Belushi in *Animal House* next to a snapped photo of a tired, grumpy sales rep just about brought the house down.

TRAINING THAT SIZZLES

Now, obviously, a sales meeting is a special occasion for the Yamaha senior leader. Over a typical workday, for instance, he can't be zapping each worker every six minutes. But Fernandez knows he should be finding ways periodically to grab their attention. And he uses product quizzes as a way to engage employees, while making learning responsibilities lighter.

"Every sales group has to have product quizzes, but we make ours fun. I announced recently that we were going to have a features quiz, and everyone groaned. But then I said that the top seven scores got to take a trip over to Krispy Kreme and get doughnuts, so everyone perked up. It's the top seven people because that's how many fit into my Ford Explorer. The winners and I drove over and got hot doughnuts. But then we also picked up 12 to 15 dozen to go and delivered them to everyone else, wearing the little Krispy Kreme hats they have. So everyone got breakfast for taking the quiz, and the people who won got to have a field trip and had a hoot doing it."

Now how easy is that? Zap!

Here's another: When Caroline Schein's team does week-long trainings for new franchisees and their teams, things can get stressful. The new restaurant is about to open, positions need to be filled, food needs to be ordered, the bank needs another hundred signatures . . . and so on. Not to mention the fact that there's a ton to learn about running a successful restaurant in that week. Frustrations run high, and attendees have little patience for other participants who come in late, use cell phones, talk too much, talk too little, act with disrespect, or just zone out.

"At the very beginning, I have the participants set the ground rules," explains Schein. "Then I'll ask, 'What should we do if someone breaks the rules that you have set? But it has to be fun.' People will suggest that the offender has to dance like Elaine from *Seinfeld* as punishment, for instance, or they have to imitate the president, or sing or overact one of our corporate values. So if someone starts monopolizing the conversation, someone will yell out, 'Box of Fun' and he or she has to reach in and take a punishment. Usually it's singing, acting, or sucking up to the facilitator. Maybe they have to get on their knees and propose marriage to the trainer. So most people are thinking, 'There's no way I want to be doing that,' and they really, really pay attention."

Another Zap!

Jim Olson, president of Harman Management, is quick to admit that he doesn't see himself as the life-of-the-party guy. But at least once a year, he steps out of his comfort zone and clowns it up. "Typically for our annual Top Ten banquet, I kind of set myself up as a bit of a joke. For instance, one year at the awards banquet it was an elaborate stage with a top-hat, formal feel, and we had professional dancers dressed up in bow ties and tails and the women were in vests and leggings. Then all the lights went out and the dancers' uniforms all had lights on them, so the audience was seeing their motions just by their lights. Then all of a sudden there's somebody that gets out on the dance floor that isn't quite as good as the rest of them. And at first, people are like, 'What's wrong with that guy?' And then the lights come on and they see it's me, and they're able to laugh and enjoy the moment because I'm making fun of my obvious lack of dancing skills."

Zap!

Olson admits the event is always fun and definitely gets people's attention. He says it makes him more human to his employees, who after the sessions become less hesitant to approach him and engage him in conversation. Many will ask, "How'd they get you to do that?" as their opening line. It's his understanding of the importance of the Levity Effect that drives him. And, this is important if you too are not the levity type, Olson is most comfortable with a more low-key approach, confessing he's not much of a funnyman. "I usually just let others sort of play off me and be their straight guy," he admits.

That's a Zap, too. Remember that great leaders are often humor appreciators rather than humor initiators. Receivers rather than givers. Catchers rather than pitchers. Shortstops rather than right fielders. So don't worry about making humor an agenda item. Simply unfurrow your brow and allow levity to stand by idling, in neutral. If the occasion arises and a sly comment is cracked, let it be. If it's funny, laugh. If you've got a nugget to add to it, toss it out there. Otherwise, give the employees initiating the levity some slack. Allow others to loosen up. When they see your jaws unclench and that you view life as so much more than dollars and cents, useful interactions and participation will multiply. Your meetings will actually accomplish something, your sales presentations will sizzle, and your learning opportunities will be so much richer.

And another bonus: people will actually want to listen to you again. How often do you find yourself with a full house on your first day of training or meetings and subsequent events are less than perfectly attended? By the time you're down to assigning actual deliverables, it seems only two of you remain. And one of them is your assistant.

HUMOROUS COMMUNICATION

Great. So, levity when properly applied in the pressure cooker of business leadership is a must-have tool. It's indispensable in nearly all forms of organizational communication.

But let's make one thing perfectly clear. Levity has its place. So does seriousness. And propriety. Concern. Patience. Discipline. While we evangelize the growing demand for lightening up in all facets of life, we also remind you to strike a fair balance, use moderation. For example, voice-mail greetings. This is an area where many of us can certainly afford to remove the cork, so to speak, and put a smile in our voice. But too many engage in long-winded comedy jams adding music and *personality*. To this approach we say, "Save it." Nobody making a phone call has time for your attempts at humor, good or disastrous. They just want to get to the beep so they can say what's on their mind. The key here is not trying to be funny, but light. In other words, you don't need to tell a joke or do your Lily Tomlin "one-ringy-dingy" impression. Just leave the greeting and be done with it.

Here's an example of someone trying too hard, a person who should learn to be jovial but not caustic. You call your paper supplier with an urgent (meaning you're in a hurry!) need to double this week's shipment. Here's the greeting on their end:

Supplier: Hey, there. You've reached Ted here at Haverly Brothers Paper Products. Sorry I can't take your call at the moment, I'm probably busy using our bathroom paper products right now.

Ha, ha. By the way, you know I used to cut down the trees for our paper, but they gave me the *axe*! Haahahahahahahaaa . . . oooooh. But anyway, when the old beeperooo goes off, do your *thang*. I'll return your call as soon as possible. So please leave a detailed message with your name and number and (sound of flushing toilet) . . . Oh! There goes the inventory! Ha, ha. (Beeeeeep.)

You: Click.

Admittedly, this example is a stretch (aren't they all?), but we've all heard greetings in this vein. Once again, the key is not to impose edgy humor in a greeting, because you have no idea who is calling that you may totally offend or alienate. Levity is the order of the day. Simply keep the tone light and informal. Here's a pretty good example. The levity is so subtle, it barely translates off the printed page:

Supplier: "Hi, you've reached John Thomas, or rather you've reached my voice mail; obviously if you'd actually reached me, we'd be talking right now. Please leave pertinent info, and I'll return your call as soon as I possibly can. Thanks."

Succinct. Nothing real serious or gut-busting there. Just a fairly straightforward, lighthearted little voice-mail greeting. It's apparent that John is just shooting from the hip, he's got a pretty good sense of humor, and he's letting it show by not taking his greeting too seriously. It is a greeting, after all. How do you greet people face to face? Stone-faced, knit-browed, and tight-lipped? Of course not. Then why greet them that way on a recording?

Now, what about e-mails or written memos? Levity can flourish through these media, but because of our fear of misunderstandings and misinterpretations we typically keep it straight, militant, boring. Far too often, this is the sort of message that arrives in our cherished in-box:

> Subject: Messes in the break room!
>
> Dear employees:
> It has come to our attention that if the current trend of not cleaning up after one's self in the break room isn't soon curtailed and/or halted, the break room will be closed until further notice. Eating on campus is a privilege, not a right.
>
> Thank you,
>
> Chizbag Kempf, Director, Corporate Privileges

This whole message smacks of a nostril-flaring jaw clencher. Ease up off the reins, big fella. A great way to lighten up with a message like this is to type it *as you would actually say it.* Reread the memo aloud, and you'll see what I mean. Nobody—not even jaw clenchers—actually talks that way. And "eating on campus"? Let's go ahead and remove the word "campus" from our workplace lexicon, shall we?

How about this instead:

> Subject: Slobs Unite!
>
> Hey everyone:
>
> I'm guessing that it won't be long before the custodial staff draws up plans for a strike. I don't even want to think about scabs crossing the picket lines, angry janitors swinging broomsticks, Molotov cocktails, etc. It's all too much. Let's just please

start picking up after ourselves in the cafeteria, and this needless violence can be averted. Thanks for your cooperation!

Chiz

Here's another missive that misses the mark:

Subject: Team Members on the Frigsten Project

Dear Team Members:

Due to the unforeseen consumption of time required to complete our deliverables for the Frigsten Project, it has become exigent that all Frigsten team associates convene until the deliverables arrive at a satisfactory state, at which point, and no sooner, will the meeting adjourn. Regardless of the hour!!! The above-mentioned meeting will begin at precisely 5:00 PM (EST). Leadership wishes to express regret if associates are inconvenienced by the potential duration of this work session.

Delwick Twitty, Project Manager

Just how difficult would it be to write something like this:

Subject: Frigsten Project Meeting

Hey everyone:

Looks like we're going to have to stay late tonight to get the Frigsten deal complete. Sorry, it could be an all-nighter. I promise to ply everyone with junk food and drinks (soda, I'm afraid, not the hard stuff). The harder we work, the sooner we can get home.

Thanks, see you at 5 PM.

Del

This e-mail isn't hilarious, but clearly comes from a manager who leads with levity. The tone of the message is serious; there's no joking when it comes to satisfying a customer. But wouldn't you be more likely to grind out a late-nighter with a positive attitude after getting this e-mail rather than the first one?

A nod to our HR friends: Written messages are *read* by their receivers, not *heard*. When you verbally toss levity around in a meeting, for example, your people can hear the tone in your voice, observe your body language and nonverbal cues that indicate that you're "just funnin'." This is not the case in an e-mail. While a levity leader will write the way he or she talks, thus making the message personal and often humorous, he or she must also read and reread it before hitting send, to make sure it is devoid of any possible misconstrueables (not an actual word, but you know what we mean).

It's also very important to note that the Levity Effect also applies in spades to *mass* internal communication vehicles—company newsletters, videos, speeches, intranet sites, and the like. We've worked with numerous corporate communication departments that face their work with such deadly seriousness, ensuring that there are no typos, grammatical errors, factual mistakes, or incorrect titles, but seem resigned to the fact that few people actually read or watch the dreadfully dull stuff they feel compelled to put out. There is a solution.

Kent Murdock, CEO of the O.C. Tanner Company, has come to understand that humor will get employees to pay attention, and he uses that information to great effect in every speech or video he's given to employees of this successful 2,000-person recognition firm. In speeches, he has rappelled from the roof into his employee crowd and has acted out the book *Who Moved My Cheese?* to help employees understand the need for a major computer system change. In company videos, he's donned an Elvis wig to show how far the company had come in its history and has even been run over by a Zamboni (a special effect) to announce the company's sponsorship of the Olympic Winter Games.

Murdock learned the art of humorous communication during his years as a trial attorney. He recalls pleading a case in a jury trial where the judge appeared to be a character plucked from a Mark Twain novel. The adjudicator wore a white linen suit and sported flowing silver hair, a bushy mustache, and designer spectacles.

Deep into the heated trial, the opposing attorney brought in a man to read the damaging testimony of a witness who had recently died. As the reader came into the courtroom, Murdock and the jury gasped. The proposed reader was the same age as the judge, dressed in the same attire, and looked like his twin brother—silver hair, bushy mustache, and the same spectacles. Obviously, the jury would be biased toward the testimony, as it would be presented by someone who was a dead ringer for the most trusted man in the room, the judge.

Bemused, Murdock stood and voiced a hopeless, "I object."

"On what grounds?" the judge asked.

Murdock paused and looked back and forth between the judge and his twin, the proposed reader.

Without missing a beat Murdock quipped, "Because he has beady eyes."

The courtroom erupted with laughter. The jury hooted. Even the judge smiled knowingly. While he allowed the reader to continue, he and the jury got the point in a memorable way that the opposing side was taking advantage of them.

The bottom line is this: Your people will be a hundred times more likely (could be more, could be less, we made it up) to follow you and produce for you, if you can simply lighten your communication up a titch. What's a titch? A skosh. We're not talking about becoming Will Ferrell. We're talking about becoming Will Marriott. Here's what he said in 1964 as he was building his hotel empire: "It's important to listen to employees, ask questions of them, say 'Good Morning' to them, ask about their families, and get to know a little bit about their aspirations, ambitions, home life, and work motivations." And buy them pizza (we added that).

That's pretty sound, practical advice from a leader who took his professional career far enough to regularly afford a new car without worrying if he spills a beverage on the upholstery. Can you do it? Set a goal for yourself that tomorrow you're going to say "good morning" to five people and ask about their families. Write it down, and do it. And remember to smile when you do it. A grumpy, perfunctory, "Mornin'. Family good?" as you pass in the break room won't knock anyone dead. We'll talk more about that later on.

Lighten up. Laugh a little. And they'll start listening. We promise.

Loosen your top button. Smile. Relax the brow. Unclench the jaw. It's just work.

SIDELIGHT
SPEAK EASY

7 PROVEN WAYS LEVITY WILL KEEP 'EM AWAKE
IN YOUR NEXT PRESENTATION

You are about to approach the podium or stage. Do you have a smile on your face and a confident twinkle in your eyes or are you quaking in your patent-leather wingtips/pumps? Here are just a few suggestions to be more effective in speeches, sales pitches, and other public appearances.

Relax

There's a reason *relax* is number one. It is, by far, the most critical step of executing a memorable, winning presentation. A few minutes before beginning, find a mirror, a window, a spoon, something with a reflection. Crack a sneaky, suspicious, devil-may-care grin at yourself, and say to yourself, "Who cares?" You **have** to relax. You **must** be calm. If you're nervous and uptight, you will not be your best. In fact, you may just stink it up. We often say to ourselves, "What are they going to do, kill us if we bomb?" Outside of actual physical pain or death, there is nothing to really worry about. (And many people don't even worry about dying; it's Thanksgiving with the in-laws they most dread.) It's that level of total relaxation that produces a calm, collected, and dead-on delivery. Being totally prepared is the easiest way to maintain relaxation. Work out all your worry the night before by pounding the material into your head, run through it 100 times if necessary, then sleep soundly. The next day go at it refreshed and unworried.

Just before you go on, replay in your head the one thing that really made you laugh in the past week or so. Remove yourself from the moment, and forget about what you're going to do. Maintain the laugh or the smile as you take the podium or laser pointer or whiteboard marker. Put the audience at ease by showing that you are at ease.

> *Typical stiff opening:* Good morning. I am pleased to be he-(ahem) here today. On behalf of the accounting department, I'd like to thank our CEO, Mr. Turdburgler, for allowing us to present for your approval the results of the annual internal audit administered by . . . blah, blah, bluey.

> *How **you'll** open:* Thanks, thanks a lot. As always it's good to be greeted by your thunderous applause cleverly disguised as apathetic silence. (They laugh.) Okay, so, I don't want to take a lot of time with this. I know it's just cold, boring numbers, and some of you look like you're already regretting not bringing a pillow . . . (they laugh again, and away you go).

Don't forget: You're just talking to people. Read that again.

You're just *talking* to *people*. You talk to people all the time. You do it all day and night. Someone probably wishes that you'd shut up at some point. It comes naturally to you because you have a tongue, teeth (at least a few remaining), lips, and an instinctive drive to communicate your need for food, shelter, and a seat in business class. You're not delivering a Pulitzer Prize acceptance speech, for heaven's sake, or addressing

Congress. Or maybe you are. Should it make a difference? We don't think so. That's why we wrote the book. So . . . *relax.* Nobody knows what you're going to say or do—except you. This is your show. You could mistakenly give your entire message backwards *in Navajo,* and no one would be the wiser. They'll just nod at each other and pretend they agree with what you're saying.

Begin with a Joke/Don't Begin with a Joke

Think of the myriad times you've sat through a presentation that blasted right out of the gate with a pretty darn good joke, and then all signs of levity quickly faded. And so did everyone's interest. Comedy almost becomes an agenda item. "Okay, top of the list, uhhh, something funny. Ummmm. A priest, a rabbi, and a minister walk into a bar. Bartender says, 'What is this, a joke?' All right. Now down to business. As you can see by the pie chart on slide one, there is a huge segment of our market that currently does not own sea lions, which flies in the face of our initial research."

If you're good at humor, go for it, but make sure the joke is timely, fresh, and somehow connected to the topic. It shouldn't be humor for humor's sake like the religious joke above. Your topic may be "Making Our Workplace Safer for All," in which case a joke about crash test dummies, worker's compensation, health care, disability, or OSHA would work nicely. But don't just launch into your spot-on but pointless impersonation of Ewan McGregor or riff on "what's up with air travel?" just to break the ice. In fact, the little bit of levity you used after you were introduced—the stuff about the lack of applause and the needing of a pillow—was a pretty decent little icebreaker without actually having to go to the joke card.

Talk to the Audience, Not at Them

Engage them in conversation as if you were just talking to someone at lunch, only louder. To that end, look at people when you talk to them. You'll naturally sound more authentic and genuine when you lock eyes with someone and just talk. Move your gaze around. See everyone. If people are obstructed from your view by inanimate objects (like columns or your CFO), move a little to be able to see their eyes. And by the way, looking just above people's heads or focusing on some far-off point on the back wall doesn't count. The audience knows what you are doing, and after all, it's a cop-out for people too insecure to be allowed out in public. Remember, once you're relaxed, this will all come easier.

Empathize with the Audience

Be constantly aware of the collective mood of the audience. Regularly and conscientiously assess how your message is being received, and adapt accordingly. Avoid monotony. Mix up the pace a little. When you see uncomfortable or bored expressions, loosen up your delivery a little or ask a question. "How's everybody? Are we doing okay? Do you have any questions at this point? Dan, you've got to be careful not to get a red mark on your forehead when you fall asleep on the table like that. You gonna make it? All right, here we go again . . ."

Set expectations of time right at the outset and occasionally give updates, "Just a few more things, then we'll wrap up . . ." or "I see I just have 10 minutes left, so I'm going to skip ahead a bit." Phrases like these are guaranteed to endear you to your listeners. They show you are well aware of what matters to these people most, getting out of this room and away from you. Nothing personal.

Add Levity

Appropriate, timely, and brief humor is the order. Understand clearly your objective, thesis, or point, and inject levity that sensibly highlights or underscores it. Your greatest ally in achieving this goal is the Internet. Google your topic or bullet point with the word "humor." You'll find jokes, quips, quotes, and an occasional image. Measure the appropriateness and, most important, applicability. Does the levity detract from or add to your message? Honestly, sometimes it just doesn't matter. Even if the link is tenuous, if it's funny and keeps people engaged, go for it. Something fun or funny every six minutes is the best rule of thumb to keep an audience paying attention through the entire presentation.

Be Human

Allow for mistakes. Laugh at your errors. But don't laugh at your jokes. If you have a technical problem, own up to it and disclose the glitch. Joke about it. You'll gain nothing by being deathly serious about it except an excruciating silence. When audiences get uncomfortable, you've lost them. Keep a smile in your eyes while presenting, but not always on your mouth. If you're smiling and laughing the whole time you'll look stupid, without a shred of credibility. But use a smile liberally. Anything that breaks out of the mold of typical, dry presentations is refreshing to audience members and memorable. Remember the second Levity Effect: if they're laughing, they're listening (and hopefully learning).

End on Time and with a Finish

No matter how great you think you're doing, when it's time to be done, be done. Leave them wanting more. They probably won't anyway. But you'll do yourself a great service, and they'll remember at least one good thing about your speech—you didn't go over time. And make sure you have an actual finish. It's a great idea to end with something funny or otherwise memorable. We nearly always end by either reiterating the moral of a story we'd previously mentioned or by wrapping the story with a second, unexpected ending. Cue a little music, summarize a few key points quickly, maybe show a humorous slide that supports your point, repeat a couple of action items (the "what are you going to *do* now that you've learned this"), then say thanks and bend over to collect the bouquets and bulls' ears you're adoring public is showering on you. Once you've "finished," then you can open it up for questions, if necessary.

CHAPTER THREE

Levity Effect— Innovation

With Comedy, There's Creativity

If you've ever tried to focus a pair of binoculars on a flying bird from a bouncing jeep, you have a slight sense of the challenges Boeing-SVS engineers tackle. The cutting-edge Boeing center in Albuquerque is dedicated to designing and building "directed energy" systems. Their designs—intricate computer programs linking laser radar, cameras, telescopes, lenses, fast-steering mirrors, gyroscopes, and GPS instruments— allow their military clients to track speeding trucks or even mortar rounds in flight, knock out a cell phone relay tower from a great distance, and can even help a flying plane identify a moving target 100 miles off and direct a beam of laser energy at it.

The math and science behind this world-changing technology happens only with a tremendous amount of creativity, engagement, and, yes, fun from the 300-person workforce.

Said site executive Lee Gutheinz, "Our motto is 'Have fun; make a difference; and oh, by the way, make a profit.' We've always told employees, 'If you're not having fun, come in and talk. We'll try to do something about it and report back.'"

Fun, said Gutheinz, drives creativity. And that innovation starts with the physical building they work in. Visitors realize the environment is light from the moment they walk through the entryway decorated with a bust of Albert Einstein wearing a bowler hat. Inside, walls are adorned with giant equations from physics, math, and business—chosen by Boeing-SVS people to enhance their areas.

"We try to create a strongly collegial atmosphere with a lot of interaction and communication," Gutheinz said. "It's very unusual to have a really great thing happen here from one person sitting down and thinking about it. Great breakthroughs tend to be ideas that have been milling around in a group of people. So when we have a big project, we'll move people from all over the building, who have widely different skills, into one area for the duration of the project. In that way, no mistake has time to propagate, and no good idea loses itself for want of an audience."

And when one of Gutheinz's teams gets stuck on a creative problem, they'll pull new people into a team room, close the door, and talk. And all conference rooms have connectivity with Boeing sites in other cities to gather some of the smartest people on the planet to help with any challenge.

It is that kind of team-oriented creativity and a parallel commitment to fun that has led Boeing-

SVS to think of new ways to tackle age-old product development problems. For example, team members often find themselves with complex prototype equipment to test. In the past, that meant moving equipment to a remote test range out of town, which meant delays in development, not to mention steep travel expenses.

Said Gutheinz, "Some of our folks needed to test a camera system that tracks missiles, but they didn't want to go to the desert of southern New Mexico to find out if it worked. So they bought a box full of toy rockets people shoot up in their backyards." He then described a safe and imaginative rigging of ropes, pillows, and pulleys the scientists and engineers devised. "Then they launched the rockets at night across the parking lot. So you had these streaking rockets shooting outside our building, and we were tracking them with our system inside the building. We drew very large crowds, and it was a lot of fun." And that fun created a very successful test, while saving the company a considerable amount of time and money.

From that first parking lot test, Boeing-SVS has now tested other equipment in their backyard. "We've developed a reputation in the local area as the crazy Boeing guys who do all these strange *Star Wars* things in the parking lot," said site executive Gutheinz. "But in the Boeing system, when people talk about us, they talk about our penchant for doing complex, lean testing. It's a characteristic of the attitude of our people to do what they need to do and have a great time doing it."

Fun at work, made even more interesting considering Boeing-SVS develops very serious aerospace products and programs. They stress quality, performance, safety, and ethics in everything they do. And yet, they also think nurturing innovation and creative problem solving through appropriate types of fun in the workplace can strengthen quality, teamwork, and performance for their customers. In short, they don't believe in fun for fun's sake, but fun that boosts creativity and very real employee engagement metrics.

In fact, for several years, Boeing-SVS consistently has been one of the top scoring sites at Boeing for employee engagement.

Questions: Do you need to develop a new product or process? Are you trying to find a solution to a particularly vexing problem? Is your company working on a new marketing or communication campaign?

The work world isn't suffering from a dearth of tedious, go-nowhere, stiff brainstorming sessions. We've all had enough of those, haven't we? Especially where just a spoonful of levity can spur the kind of breakout success we've seen as a result of conjuring clever and creative ideas. But you don't have to just trust us: Research shows that you can boost scores on a standardized test of creativity by exposing people to humor or other conditions that establish a "playful atmosphere."

"If you can find a job where you have fun, it will feel like a calling," said Dave Clark, HR vice president of sports-apparel giant Nike. "If you can find that zone, where you have such a passion for the job that it becomes fun, you are in the sweet spot for creativity."

Basically, there are three ways to get to that sweet spot: (1) Make the work environment more fun;

(2) Expose and awaken latent funness (not a word) from more serious employees; and, if number two doesn't work; (3) Hire employees who are more fun and creative.

MAKE WORK MORE FUN
AND CREATIVE

One of us had a neighbor who came home from his office job every day at five. He climbed off the bus, ripped off his constricting tie, and spent two hours with his miniature gas-powered aircraft. In his garage tinkering or out on the school playground flying, his countenance came alive with the passion of his hobby.

Like this neighbor, most employees are passionate about something—fishing, gardening, nose rings—just not their jobs. Finding and tapping into that passion can fire up employee creative juices.

Now, some companies are lucky; their people are rabid aficionados of their products or services. We worked with a group of managers recently at Cabela's, the renowned sporting goods retail superstore, in Sydney, Nebraska. Cabela's has stores the size of an IKEA, but they sell fishing rods rather than Swedish curtain rods. Their sports superstores are so huge, they can be seen from Neptune (even without the latest in superpowerful hunting scopes—available at Cabela's!).

The vast majority of employees at Cabela's were already passionate about the outdoors when they came aboard. From accountants to cashiers and hunting specialists to alpaca stuffers, the employees really dig what they do, and that passion translates into more fun, which in turn boosts their bottom line. Lots of organizations enjoy the same good fortune.

"Here at Nike, we're about sports," Clark told us. "We try our best to live in the world of athletics."

Understanding its customers' obsession with competition, Nike leadership approaches business like a sport, enabling employees to feel the thrill of corporate competition and the high of winning big.

"Each quarter when we announce our results to Wall Street, we have a company meeting where our senior leadership shares the news, and then we celebrate after," said Clark. "We go out and mingle. We have live music, food, contests, refreshments. Overall, we want employees to feel the corporate competition and know that we're winning. Winning is fun."

That's not the kind of shocking news we'd interrupt *Dancing with the Stars* to report, but it's good to be reminded: Winning is fun.

Now, to spur the kind of creativity that leads to a win, it's not unusual for Nike to send its people to far-flung places to get them into a creative mind-set. Employee groups might attend an athletic competition, such as the Boston Marathon or the National Hockey League All-Star Game; they might get a sense of what's cool in attire by hanging out at a skate park in New York or riding the waves with the surf dudes at Redondo Beach. But, they might also do something seemingly unrelated to sports, but still enjoyable, just to spur creativity. For instance, they've visited movie sets, sat through a taping of *Oprah*, and have even climbed the breathtaking Sydney Harbor Bridge.

Clark explains that it's about going where the energy is and watching for what's hot—in their industry and outside their world.

Advertising executive Linda Kaplan Thaler says creativity in her agency has come from reducing command and control management. Even though her organization has annual revenues exceeding $1 billion, she runs her company like a fun team writing a sitcom.

"We don't have groups, we don't have fancy titles, we don't pay people according to the number of people they supervise but by the quality of the work they produce and the business they bring into the agency," she explained. "Part of creativity in the workplace is creating an atmosphere where people feel safe. People are spending an awful lot of time here, so you've got to get people to really like and trust each other."

She explains that creativity is hard work, and great creative meetings allow people to loosen up and become more imaginative. "So many good ideas are born out of someone else's bad idea. But if people don't feel warmth and humor in the room, they aren't going to throw out an idea in the first place.

"The idea isn't to get just the good ideas out, but to get all of the ideas out. Even if an idea is a turkey, you kid around about it. 'Like the client will ever buy that.' We've won a lot of accounts with ideas that people might have been afraid to raise their hands with."

For example, the Kaplan Thaler Group recently created a promotion on breast cancer awareness for the Lifetime Network. The Group had a nugget of an idea: To remind people of the need to be supportive of those who were going through the disease, but also to get those people to lighten up a bit. It was a project close to home for Kaplan Thaler, who had suffered from breast cancer years before when she worked at J Walter Thompson.

"When I came back to work everybody was afraid to say anything to me, and they all gave me these soulful looks. It was exactly what I *didn't* want. Finally, we were in a meeting, and someone sneezed, and another person moved away, apologizing that they didn't want to get a cold. I said, 'You don't have to move away from me because you really can't catch what I have.' Everyone looked at me, and I had to tell them, 'It's okay to laugh.' Humor helps you get through a lot."

So, that was the idea for the breast cancer campaign. To not only raise awareness of being supportive, but to lighten the mood of those suffering. The Group brought together a creative team, including a young intern who had only recently graduated from college. It was her first brainstorming session, and she was obviously afraid to speak up to the creative geniuses who had worked on some of the world's most successful ad campaigns. But Kaplan Thaler and her team begged and cajoled the young woman into sharing an idea . . . any idea.

Recalls Kaplan Thaler, "The intern said, 'This may be totally crazy, but when my friends and I sign off on our e-mails to each other, we always end it with *You are my bra.* It means you're my support, my lift. It's probably too crazy, I can't believe I just said that.'"

That crazy idea turned into the Lifetime Network's national breast cancer awareness campaign, "Be my support. Be my strength. Be my bra." From a simple thought from a quiet participant came a "Be My Bra" song, a series of TV commercials starring Whoopi Goldberg, and a print and web campaign.

"It became this huge thing," said Kaplan Thaler. "Why? Because we were kidding around, creating an atmosphere that was very light, a lot of fun, very friendly, and we said don't be inhibited. Share any crazy idea. Think if this woman had never been invited to a meeting or never raised her hand, or hadn't felt comfortable in sharing. We wouldn't have a campaign that was so much fun."

Now, you may not have Kaplan Thaler's world-class sense of humor or be able to send your employees to Australia to get better ideas and creativity, but there are some simple things you can do to lighten up brainstorming meetings to get creativity flowing. One of us worked for a company that began each idea meeting with a hot fresh pizza and a cock-and-bull session. We chatted, caught up on current events, and laughed a lot. Barbs were exchanged. Stories were shared. The Heimlich was performed. All good fun. Then the ideas really flowed. Mostly unexpected, *out-of-the-box* creativity, born of innocent levity.

Here are some ideas to get the ball rolling:

- Before the meeting, take a few minutes to watch some especially witty and clever TV ads or look at a few imaginative magazine ads to get minds in the right, creative frame.

- Keep a stack of toys, puzzles, Nerf balls, balsa airplanes, Slinky toys, and Silly Putty in meeting rooms. To play with of course, not just for adornment.

- Cover the table with white paper and give everyone colored pencils or crayons to draw out the problem.

- Let people dress casually and meet in a place with natural light.

- Have candy and water available and buy lunch.

- Take a quick break every hour to do something physical and fun—spin in your chairs a half dozen times; tell your worst clean joke; get up and dance as badly as possible; stand and recite the company mission statement using your best impressions; rhyme every phrase for a few minutes; play a round of charades, 20 questions, Pictionary, and so on.

- After the project is over, get back together to celebrate.

- Then, have another quick meeting with your team to simply agree that you'll take the time to have fun again in other meetings . . . and ask for their help in lightening up.

Incorporating fun into the situation solved a problem for Ross Environmental Services. They were having a difficult time getting employees to attend their annual (yawn) awards banquet and ceremonies. You've probably attended one of these yourself. It's the time equivalent of a Ken Burns film, but with one-seventh the excitement. They're sometimes held off-site at an Elk's Lodge or the back room of a Shoney's. The company was dedicating a lot of its resources to these affairs and had kept it very dignified, thinking it would mean more to their employees.

Who wants *dignified?* You're bringing me to dinner and a celebration of some kind, and I end up face down in my bowl of broccoli-and-cheese soup snoring loud enough to wake the dead?

At last, with attendance worsening (think Nielsen ratings for the final season of *Facts of Life*), the company decided to break with tradition and wrap their award party around a concept not often associated with dignified: Casino Night.

"The RSVPs were out of control," said CEO Art Hargate. "Our thought process was, we'll of course do the same awards: the recognition is very important to people, but we'll just make the whole thing more fun. It really got people to come out, and that's the whole point—bringing as much of the team together as possible to celebrate who we are and what we've achieved."

See? They still meted out well-deserved recognition, shook hands, took photos, and butchered some last names on a PowerPoint slide. But now, everyone was grateful to be there. A little fun—and by fun of course we mean *gaming*—made all the difference.

As effective and fun as corporate-sponsored events can be, Clark at Nike understands that one of the best things they can do as leaders to boost creativity is simply to be relaxed enough to allow employees to create their own fun.

"Part of our culture here is that we have a company radio talk show called KAOS. Every Thursday morning, people can sit at their desks and click on the link. It's really not politically correct stuff. You hear what people are thinking, but are afraid to say. It just started and grew and grew. It's now expanded to reach all of our offices. It wasn't something leadership sponsored, but management supports it because it's part of our innovative culture. We don't want to shut down fun because we'll end up shutting down creativity."

And that's the key, really. Sometimes the best way to increase creativity is to simply discontinue telegraphing disapproval of employee levity. Unknit your eyebrows. Declench your jaws a little.

Said one employee who participated in our research: "A 'fun' work environment is where people don't take themselves too seriously, especially supervisors and managers, while getting their work done. You can work hard and have fun at the same time. But if leadership is too strict and tries to have fun, it comes off like 'Funny Hat Day' at the Springfield Nuclear Power Plant on *The Simpsons.* The workers are first shown in various states of depression. The next day they are the same sad bunch, but hey, they're wearing funny hats."

David Vik, the coach at Zappos.com, which has grown gross merchandise sales from almost nothing to more than $600 million in less than nine years, has noticed that employees who are freed up to enjoy their work do their best work. That's the philosophy and culture we're talking about and the one that the Zappos phenomenon was built on, which now has more than six million fanatical customers.

"Employees just aren't their most creative when they're micromanaged or in an overly structured environment. People do better work when they're more relaxed. Zappos.com is tethered to a brilliant infrastructure—hire skilled and talented people and allow them to do what they do. And many times, they come up with something better than we could have hoped for, just by letting them create. So our leaders not only allow some fun, but also take the initiative when stress is high to lighten things up, helping to resume a more relaxed and creative atmosphere."

The key to encouraging innovation within the ranks of the Virgin Group (the company), suggests owner and founder Richard Branson, is to create a lighter environment where managers listen to any and all ideas. Employees often leave companies, he says, because they are frustrated by the fact that their ideas fall on deaf ears. Interaction between employees and managers is fundamental. For the companies in which he serves as both chief executive and chairman, Branson writes his staff what he calls fun "chitty-chatty" letters to tell them everything that is going on and to encourage them to write him with any ideas or suggestions. He gives them his home address and phone number. He responds with a letter personally, even if he doesn't follow up and deal with the details. Sometimes people come to him with personal problems, while others have suggestions for improvements in their companies. Either way, they get the chance to be heard . . . by a billionaire, no less.

Employees at Boston Pizza regularly are encouraged to take time to "monkey" around, especially when doing creative work, said Caroline Schein. "I was on a team with really long, long hours with no end in sight. Over time, productivity and creativity started to decline. So we pulled the team together and said, 'What do we need to do to turn this around?' The team came up with a mascot named Roman, a little stuffed monkey that roamed around the world. Whoever got to escape on holiday had to take Roman. He even got arrested once, which was a blast to hear about."

Also on their own initiative, employees started sending out "Golden Bananas" to each other, honoring colleagues who were "having fun while being the best." The whole thing worked, said Schein, first because it was initiated by employees and second because management was loose enough to let it happen—they lead with levity. Oh, and by the way, Boston Pizza has enjoyed 18 percent annual growth over the last 10 years, including a whopping 25 percent growth in revenue in 2006.

The top concern among your average brow-knitting leader in allowing employee-sponsored fun to spur creativity is that it usually involves giving latitude and discretion to the workforce. That can be a tough pill for some highly structured leaders to swallow (without hiding it in a spoonful of applesauce). We can't help but think of these types of leaders standing over employees with a stopwatch, yelling "Laugh! Damn you, laugh! We need that new idea." Of course, the concept is ludicrous. Really! Who owns a stopwatch anymore?

Here's a simple example of fun that inspires longer-term performance: Root Learning in Sylvania, Ohio, creates caricatures of employees when they join the consulting firm. As the years go by, coworkers add details to each drawing, reflecting the employee's interests, quirks, and their innovative contributions to the job. As the pictures evolve, they reflect a growing understanding of the individual. On the eighth year, a personalized background is added by a company artist.

Employees at another company turned a file room into an impromptu obstacle course, transforming a chore into a game. Employees at yet another firm dreaded opening the huge stack of daily mail until they began hiding gift certificates for each other in the stacks.

"We understand that structure dictates function, but that structure doesn't need to be overbearing," said Dr. Vik of Zappos.com. "Instead of telling people what to do—and then when they've finished, saying 'Now what?'—we allow them the liberty to be creative and see what they come up with. That way, you end up with people taking ownership in their jobs, which ultimately means less management than the traditional way of doing business.

"Our leaders don't tell employees how to do it. They let them know what needs to be done and then let them do it."

At work, create flexibility, encourage fun, get out of your comfort zone, and the ideas will start to flow.

GETTING SERIOUSAHOLICS TO BE MORE CREATIVE

Creative people are different in that they make connections between ideas or events that others can see only when they're pointed out. Humor works in the same way. To *get* a joke, you have to find some unexpected meaning, requiring lateral or divergent thinking, both of which are higher-level thinking skills. Such thinking involves a shift away from the usual way of looking at things and primes the creative juices.

That's why even just sitting down and watching a comedy is enough to significantly improve creative problem solving, according to data published in the *Journal of Personality and Social Psychology*. (Not exactly world-changing research, but hey.)

Think for a minute about your favorite funny film. Does it really get you squealing with laughter?

When you find yourself completely devoid of good ideas and creativity, pop your movie in and watch a little. Scott has a copy of *This Is Spinal Tap,* and sometimes he just has to cue up his favorite bits. For Adrian, Chevy Chase's *Funny Farm* induces cackles and howls of laughter, which refreshes the senses and helps get ideas flowing. A little humor increases creativity by leaps and bounds.

Another of our favorite comedies is *What About Bob?* starring Bill Murray. If you've seen it, you'll remember that Murray's paranoid, delusional, multiphobic character, Bob, had to take "baby steps" to overcome his problems. "Baby steps across the room. Baby steps to the elevator," he would mutter to himself.

It's not a bad mantra for leaders who want to improve their employees' creativity levels by using humor and levity. It's not necessary or wise to attempt to overhaul the mood around the office in one fell swoop. Over time, small steps can result in big improvements, as Dr. Vik can tell you. As the coach of Zappos.com, he has seen many take their personal and business lives to the next level by taking such baby steps. "At Zappos, we provide one-on-one coaching with our employees. We start off by having employees choose a 30-day goal in whatever area of their lives they want to take to the next level. I have seen people buying houses, saving money, losing weight, exercising more, getting promoted, and much more.

"Many times we just keep doing what we're doing, and we don't stop to get creative and see where we want to be in the future. It all starts with what we call a 30-day goal. It's so unbelievable to see all the people who are winning in their own lives around here. We all go around slapping high fives."

Baby steps.

Hargate, CEO of Ross Environmental Services, understands how that works.

"The regulatory environment is very strict, and there are potentially big penalties if you mess up. Our customers expect us to be very serious people. So lightening up for us is hard. . . . Being serious-aholics, it's like a 12-step program. You have to take it one day at a time."

Bringing levity to the conference room table can be as simple as playing a quick round of hangman to help employees stretch their thinking and look at problems from a different perspective. In many ad firms and other creative enterprises we visited, employees begin meetings discussing the task or problem at hand, then they'll take a *toy break*, where they are each given a plaything and are asked to consider how the Slinky, Bionicle, or Barbie Dream House relates to solving the task. Each toy takes the employee's thinking in a different direction.

Along these lines, the Yamaha Marine Division has raced paper boats in a hotel pool to promote team building and creativity. Norton Healthcare has had Elvis deliver patient meals. Even something as straightforward as waiting on tables can be approached with more fun and creativity, as evidenced by casual dining chain Boston Pizza.

"For example, if we have a Rib-Rageous promotion, everyone can wear western attire and cowboy hats," said VP Schein. "Employees really get into it. We also have draws during sporting events and have different jerseys for the football season. The goal is that employees will have fun with the guests, but the fun is also to help them get creative in their selling approach during promotions."

Here's another example of fun driving sales, while helping this organization give back to the community: For years, Boston Pizza has partnered with the Heart and Stroke Foundation to run a systemwide promotion every Valentine's Day. On that special day, the chain sells heart-shaped pieces of paper for two dollars. Guests write their names on the cards and affix them to the walls, and all the proceeds go directly to the Foundation. But there's a twist.

The company also sells heart-shaped pizzas that day.

Now, we have no research to prove this, but if you asked most women what they'd like for Valentine's Day, the list would probably include jewelry, flowers, and a gift certificate to Nordstrom's. You'd be hard pressed to add a pizza pie to the list. ("I hope he remembers the olives!")

But do you know what the number-one sales day is for Boston Pizza every year? February 14.

Said Schein, "It's a huge, huge day, with wait times for delivery in excess of two hours, but guests don't seem to mind. Some restaurants just raise amazing amounts of money for the Foundation. And it's something that helps our employees feel good about working and making a contribution to something bigger. Our employee demographics are definitely younger. If you think about Generation Y they want to make a difference more than many other generations."

That's the payoff. Fun gives employees more creative ways to interact with the guests, creating a unique—and winning—company.

Now *that's* fun—winning.

HIRE PEOPLE WHO ARE
MORE CREATIVE

This may be the simplest approach to building some levity into your workplace: Weed out the gravely serious early on in the process.

Now, we're not suggesting you take a "qualifications, schmalifications" stance, and only hire for humor. After all, who wants an office full of under-qualified shtick comics and funmakers lollygagging about? But we are talking about finding the fun-minded because they are usually smarter and easier to work with, and customers love them.

"If you look around here, we let people be themselves," said Dr. Vik. "People who work here have to be fun. We have tattooed people—people in slippers, people with orange and pink hair. We have dolls in cubes, posters hanging on the ceiling. I've even got a chicken on my desk because the guy across from me has a chicken, and he claims it's the best chicken around. But it doesn't make a noise. So I hunted down a chicken that just kills his chicken. Little things like that are fun."

But, he warns, no one said it's easy.

Over the years, Vik has come to understand a universal truth: While you can help employees be more creative, building a fun and creative culture is easiest if you start out with fun and creative people to begin with.

That's what Herb Kelleher, retired CEO of South-west Airlines, was looking for when he hired people. He said, "What we are looking for, first and foremost, is a sense of humor. . . . We don't care much about education and expertise because we can train peo-ple. . . . We hire attitudes."

Likewise for Amy Miller, CEO of the franchise Amy's Ice Cream. Her stores have stopped giving out formal application forms. Instead, they hand out paper bags. "You are asked to do something creative with it while including at least your name and phone number," she says.

Miller adds that one bag came back attached to a helium balloon, made to look like the basket of a hot air balloon. Another applicant turned the bag into an aquarium complete with live goldfish. Another person pasted pictures of her accomplishments on the outside.

"The application bag is pretty effective at weed-ing out applicants who probably wouldn't fit into the company culture anyway," she says.

At ad giant, the Kaplan Thaler Group, Linda Kaplan Thaler believes in hiring the humorous, so much so that lately she's hired a few stand-up comics to write ad copy.

"I always look to see how funny somebody is be-cause it's so indicative of their intelligence," she said. "It says a lot about a person: That they don't take themselves too seriously, and that they can make disparate connections, which is the essence of creativity and humor. Freud wrote a book called *The Joke and Its Relation to the Unconscious*. . . . He wasn't a great title writer. But in the book he talks about humor being the ability of the brain to put un-like elements together, like a dog praying in church. People without a sense of humor aren't seeing those weird connections, which we use in advertising."

But how do you hire fun people when humor in the workplace strikes its intended targets in such diverse ways? As we travel and give addresses and presentations, audiences reactions vary, as you would expect. Some are guffawing. Others chortle. Snicker. Giggle. A few blow beverages from their nostrils. Some have even admitted to soiling themselves. And yet, there's always a few people scattered throughout with confused, stunned, or indifferent expressions on their faces. (Only a few, mind you, we are brilliant speakers.)

The fact is, there is not a single bit of mirth that strikes two people exactly the same way. Your friend is reading an article in the newspaper and laughing uncontrollably. Red face, tears, the whole production. Your curiosity piqued, you grab the paper with a smile of anticipation for the therapy this good laugh will give you. You read the joke/cartoon/editorial/obituary and your reaction is far less dramatic than that of your friend. You nod and smile and politely say, "Hmm. That's funny." Meanwhile your friend is hooking up to an oxygen tank.

Thank heavens there is not a Laugh Enforcement Department. We can just see the Laugh Cops breaking down our door and hauling us away in cuffs because we found last night's *Tonight Show* monologue a little gimpy.

Sgt. Chuckles: "We understand you didn't care for the whole bit about the Speaker of the House.

Stop squirming; the cuffs won't hurt. You didn't laugh at all?"

Us: "There was nothing funny about it."

Officer Giggles: "Not funny, huh? Why don't you make this easy on yourself?"

(We are thrown across the hood of their "Clown" Victoria and pummeled with whoopee cushions and rubber chickens.)

So in a world where no one shares your exact sense of humor, how do you hire for levity? Leaders who manage with the Levity Effect tell us repeatedly that they go into an interview looking for simple things: a smiling face, a positive attitude, and an open personality.

According to Nina McVey, assistant vice president of human resources at Enterprise Rent-A-Car, "We have a culture, and we hire folks who naturally want to enjoy themselves and have a good time, and they tend to be upbeat and assertive. We say, 'If you're not having fun, you shouldn't be doing what you're doing.' The person has to have core competencies, of course, but it's also how they carry themselves and present themselves. If in an interview they can poke fun at themselves rather than stress out, I tend to think they're pretty well balanced and can think on their feet."

Tim Fernandez, general manager of sales for the Yamaha Marine Division Outboard Group in Atlanta, says, "When we are sitting down and interviewing, we want to find someone who fits the mold of the rest of us. We're all hard workers, we enjoy our product and have a sense of pride in what we do, but we also have some sort of sense of humor. We look for that in an interview. It comes across if people are open and smiling, and it makes a great impression on us. Even if they are nervous, they can still be trying to smile and open up; that's okay too. We try to loosen them up by cracking a little joke about something and trying to make them feel at ease. We are not always funny, but if they respond to it, it's very good. If they are trying to come across so serious, it might be a red flag."

Craig Kerkove, senior vice president and general manager of the Semiconductor Equipment Division of Hitachi High Technologies America, works hard to find lighthearted supervisors or managers. "We'll ask them to give us some examples of really fun things they've done to keep their employees energized and motivated. People who aren't trying to blow smoke will pretty quickly mention two or three things they've done in the past. You try to drill down in that way by asking, 'What have you done to make the job fun for yourself and for others?'" Screenings such as these have kept turnover in his division to less than 3 percent annually.

Others take hiring for levity a bit further, asking all potential employees specific questions designed to bring out a person's sense of humor. (See the Side-Light for more details.) And others are even willing to pass over people who may be competent but lack a sense of humor.

"We have people who come through to interview who are technically sound, maybe even brilliant, but they won't get the job if they are too stuffy, if they can't chitchat with people easily," says Schein of Boston Pizza. "We are looking for people who are outgoing, quick with a smile, who can work with fellow employees and guests.

"In some places I've worked, they may say that they seek personality, but honestly, it's just words. They hire the uptight people. What they say and what they do are opposite."

Hargate with Ross Environmental Services admits that holding out for just the right person can absolutely transform a department or a company.

"I hired a controller a few years ago. We had real trouble finding the right person, but we found this guy, and he has a really good sense of humor. For the first time working here in 18 years . . . really, 18 years . . . it's the first time I've actually heard the people in his department laugh out loud. They're much more relaxed. Nothing fazes this guy, and so nothing fazes his staff. And what is more serious than accounting? What could be more deadly? But with a good, wry sense of humor, he keeps his people loose, and it's very healthy."

A quick review. So far, we've found levity boosts *productivity, communication,* and *creativity.* Those are some pretty rich payoffs from the department of Not Too Shabby just for lightening and loosening up. Now, if only fun could make you a more trusted and admired businessperson. Read on to the next chapter.

SideLight
Employing Levity

8 Questions to Determine
a New Employee's Fun Potential

We often ask business leaders this simple question: Who is more dangerous to your firm—the new hire who is incompetent or the new hire who doesn't fit your culture? It may seem like a simple answer because the incompetent person can seemingly cause a lot of damage, right? If they make a mistake, you could send out the wrong order, sell something for less than cost, divert the shipment to Tucson instead of Tuscaloosa, amputate the wrong body part (use a Sharpie for goodness' sake). . . . But in reality, a good boss typically can spot an incompetent employee by lunchtime on the first day. And they are gone. Someone who doesn't fit your culture? That can take much, much longer to discover, and by then, the damage may be done to customer relationships, team morale, and productivity.

While most leaders spend the vast majority of time in an interview identifying a candidate's competencies, great managers spend an equal amount of time judging the character, fit, and good humor of their potential hires—realizing that a buoyant new hire can literally change a work environment for the better.

First, before you even start interviewing, make sure a sense of humor is a requirement on the job posting itself. And don't be afraid to use some fun phrases on the want ad to grab attention. For example, we once helped write a description for an important customer service position at a large bank. Leaders were having difficulty attracting the right person. After an edit, the ad started out with the lines, "Here at our bank, we're a pretty hip bunch. Sure, we all wear uncomfortable clothes and pepper our conversations with phrases like, 'Capital Allocation,' 'Risk Management,' and 'Hey, who's taken all the Form 32-B-8745s?' But despite our shortcomings, we believe in having fun, and we want the right person to help us lighten up and provide outrageously great service to our clients." Two hundred applications later, they quickly closed the posting with an amazingly qualified woman who was a spark to the entire organization.

Next, after you shake hands with a potential new hire, put things in context by explaining how employees at your organization not only work hard, but have a good time. "Here at Solid Waste Management and Toothpaste Concern, fun is not just a slogan, it's really how we run our business." Explain that you are looking for people who have a passion for their work, a sense of humor, and whose light attitudes are contagious. Then it's time for them to shine. What follows are eight questions that you can ask to help identify a potential levity-minded employee or leader:

1. Tell me about a time you used humor or a lighter tone to diffuse a difficult situation.

2. How have you used your wit to win over an audience, maybe in selling a product or making a big presentation?

3. If we asked former bosses about you, would they say you're a fun person? Why or why not?

4. Explain your overall philosophy of having fun at work.

5. What's the most fun event or activity that you've ever participated in at work?

6. If you could create your perfect work environment, what would it be like?

7. Your manager has asked you to come up with a creative solution to a problem. Understanding that we believe fun spurs creativity, how would you get started on tackling the problem?

8. Tell me how you would bring fun and energy to our company.

CHAPTER FOUR

Levity Effect— Respect

In You They Trust

Michael Jewellson is a miracle worker.

We met this mild-mannered gentleman on a visit to the Norton Healthcare system in Louisville, Kentucky. Jewellson is the director of food and nutrition for Morrison Management Specialists assigned to Norton Audubon Hospital, one of the nation's finest heart hospitals. On a typical day he will serve up to 2,000 meals. His team of 60 serves 60,000 meals each month. But that's not the miracle; that's business as usual.

Before he took over as director of food and nutrition for the hospital, its ranking on courtesy of food service personnel couldn't have been any lower. Nationally, the department was ranked among the lowest in the nation with just 1 percent approval on customer-courtesy scores. Essentially, that meant the patients would rather have been served by a farm animal than an actual employee.

The CEO of Norton Healthcare was proud to share the turnaround story. He explained that within six months of Jewellson's arrival on the job, the food and nutrition department at Norton Audubon Hospital had skyrocketed to the 99th percentile in courtesy in a national ranking. Performance also increased significantly in quality of food served, employee satisfaction, and other criteria.

But from 1 percent to 99 percent in six months? Jewellson's either a magician, a genius, or there was some kind of computational error in the original survey. Nope, he just knows something you should know.

When we met Jewellson to discover his secrets, he was quick to deflect the praise onto his managers and team.

"Do you have different employees now than those who had the 1 percent ranking?" we asked, wondering if he simply jettisoned all the old, underperforming employees.

"A few, but most are the same."

"Well then, Michael, you might have made the difference. What did you do?"

Reluctantly he explained that it started with building respect.

"When I came here, the negativity was so thick you could cut it with a knife," he explained. "So we made a conscious effort to be positive with everything. We started showing each and everyone respect, listening to them, thanking them. And we started stressing that we should have fun at work."

Jewellson's department quickly got a reputation for having too much fun. "People would walk by, hear this hysterical laughter coming from our offices, and they'd want to know what was going on. We took courteous service very seriously, but everything else had to be fun."

He explained, "We quit dwelling on the squeaky wheel who gets the oil and started respecting the high performers, giving them more attention in our daily line-up meetings, explaining the good things they were doing. And that started bringing everyone else up to their level. It shifted our focus from the complainers to the high performers. When they started getting respect for what they'd done, it changed the mind-set of what everyone was doing."

Pretty soon the respect and positive vibe started spreading throughout the department and the entire hospital, and employees were happy to buy in. It started in small ways—a smile at patients or cafeteria customers—and soon employees began suggesting new menu items, then they were volunteering to pitch in and help on banquets.

One day, the retail manager took Jewellson at his word and dressed up as Elvis and visited the cafeteria. Instead of getting in trouble for rocking the boat, he was celebrated. And a trend was started. Soon, another manager dressed up as a school nerd for Back-to-School Days, complete with propeller beanie, thick glasses, short pants, suspenders, and obnoxious striped shirt. In July, yet another employee dressed up as Santa Claus and made an appearance for Christmas in July.

Jewellson would take time to visit with heart patients and their families. He'd joke that his cooking wasn't as good as at home, but then ask for feedback on how he was doing. Then his chef started making rounds too in his tall white hat, telling patients that he wouldn't do any doctoring as long as the doctor wasn't doing any cooking.

"We got out of the business of serving meals and got into the business of helping heal patients," said Jewellson. "And that's a lot more fun."

When the survey scores came in and Norton Audubon reached 99 percent on customer courtesy, Jewellson and his managers had to find an amusing way to celebrate with the people who did the work. Naturally.

"To show appreciation for the entire staff, we made a five-star restaurant meal in the cafeteria and hand-waited on our employees. We used fine china, linen. We used it as our monthly department meeting and had a huge turnout. We served beef tenderloin and shrimp, and we had a great time."

Says Jewellson, "You can't have too much fun at work. The happier your employees are the healthier they are. I don't want to slow down the momentum that we have here.

"We use humor a lot. And that is built from respect. When everyone is together it's very informal and everyone gets a chance to speak. Sure, there's always someone who is mad at the world, but we even try to make light of that. And if that behavior doesn't change, we just don't tolerate it."

If you observed Jewellson at work, you may think his methods of lightening up in the world of food service may seem a little severe to some in more genteel surroundings. For example, Jewellson will walk into one of his kitchens and, as he says, start talking trash.

"My production staff are the hardest workers, and it's 100 degrees in the kitchen. So you've got to go in there and pick them up. I'll give them a hard time and get them going. I'll joke that I could outcook them blindfolded. They don't hold back. They fire stuff back at me, and I always let them smoke me on the jabs, which isn't hard. It's a whole lot of fun."

HUMOR EARNS SOME RESPECT

Think of levity not simply as a tool in the workplace, but a symptom of its culture. The conditions necessary to make a joke effective are the same conditions necessary to make a business work: communication, understanding, common ground, trust, and respect. And surprisingly, interpersonal relationships that grow out of these environments are almost completely disregarded as too soft by many leadership consultants, business gurus, and even by managers who seek to improve how their organizations function.

The Boeing Company has been surveying its employees since the 1950s. The 2007 employee survey had more than 100,000 respondents for a 75 percent response rate. Ruth Savolaine, Employee Relations Communications Manager at Boeing, said leaders at one site noted a surprising discovery from focus groups conducted after the 2005 survey, "We saw that managers who scored the highest on a dozen different engagement questions were simply better at doing the little, respectful things that employees appreciated. They asked employees how their weekends were; they asked about their kid's soccer game; they went to their employee's office space instead of requiring them to come to their office. They lived the Golden Rule—treat others as you would have them treat you."

Our findings echo this emphasis on respect. As we were interviewing executives on the subject of levity, we didn't expect the concept of respect to arise so frequently, but great leaders knew instinctively that it was directly related to the ability to have fun. And the Great Place to Work® Institute research backs this up. It seems you can't have fun if respect between colleagues doesn't exist. Greater amounts of respect build greater amounts of trust. And trust leads to an environment where fun can flourish. You follow that? The imperative need for respect emerged as a dominant need in every single interview we conducted. And one tangible demonstration of respect, according to all the effective leaders we spoke with, was the need to roll up your sleeves and work with employees.

Says Jewellson at Norton Audubon Hospital: "I'm not the kind of director who sits and directs. I'm involved in 90 percent of the caterings, whether setting up or helping cook. I let them see that I'm willing to do whatever they are willing to do. It's not beneath me to take off my tie and wash some pots and pans."

When was the last time you rolled up your metaphorical sleeves, slipped off your metaphorical tie, and metaphorically washed pots and pans with your employees? Metaphorically speaking, of course.

In stressful environments (the workplace, doctor's office, cell block C), respect and trust help alleviate pressure. Great leaders simply show a lot of respect for their people. But sadly, many employees we spoke with say they feel invisible. And it's hard to laugh when you think or feel that way.

Virgin Group owner and founder Richard Branson said that bosses overcome this by making respectful connections with employees not only at work, but also while leaning up against a bar. "Some 80 percent of your life is spent working," he said. "You want to have fun at home; why shouldn't you have fun at work? I think leaders have got to make a bigger effort to make sure the people who work for them are enjoying what they're doing. If a chairman of a company visits Seattle, that chairman should take all the staff out in the evening, have a few drinks together, talk together, party together, and not be embarrassed about the staff seeing your weaker side. They don't lose respect for you because they see your human side. They actually gain more respect for you."

Branson and other levity leaders will tell you that treating employees with closeness and dignity is also critical in retention efforts. Those employees who feel like they are not respected by their employers are much more likely to leave their jobs. According to a recent Sirota survey, employees are three times more likely to leave their employers within two years if they do not feel respected—63 percent of respondents to the survey planned to exit within two years compared with only 19 percent who sensed respect.

There is also a strong correlation between respect and employee engagement. In the Sirota survey, those who described themselves as feeling "very good" about their treatment by employers were three times more enthusiastic about their work than those who described themselves as feeling just "good" about the way they were treated.

"The data clearly supports what many employees feel: Nonmanagement employees are treated with less respect than management (especially senior management)," Douglas Klein of Sirota said. "While almost half of senior-level managers feel they are shown a great deal of respect, just one-quarter of supervisors and only one-fifth of nonmanagement employees feel the same way. In fact, one out of every seven nonmanagement employees actually feels they are treated poorly or very poorly."

It's telling that a 2006 survey revealed nearly half of all health-care workers said they'd "begun to think about or make plans to leave their current organization," and 55 percent of primary care physicians under the age of 45 will leave their current practice in the next four years. "After 15 years as a physician executive," wrote David Epstein, MD, of Marietta, Georgia, "I am profoundly disappointed at the treatment afforded medical directors, nursing executives, and other clinical professionals by nonclinical management executives. . . . It's about honesty and respect—two qualities in very short supply."

Poor treatment of employees exists in every industry. The conditions tend not to be extreme or abusive, as a rule. The stories most likely to make it to the front page are criminal acts, but the majority of dissatisfied employees say their unhappiness is due to a lack of proper, respectful behavior. They want common courtesy, basic civility. Their *props* as it were. But management is too often indifferent to them. Employees fade into the background, invisible to almost all leadership.

The scale of respectful acts can be small and still have a big effect. "When I look at what we do here, it's a lot of little things that add up to a good environment," says Tim Fernandez, general manager of sales, Yamaha Marine Division Outboard Group in Atlanta, Georgia. "For example, this is a little thing, but every year we print up T-shirts for our dealers as a gift. We design them to represent various things from fishing to waterskiing. We make sure employees get them too. It's a small act, but it's a huge thing to them. Most organizations wouldn't worry about that, but those little things show our people respect.

"When you are the manager and you can sit back and look at what your employees are doing and demonstrate to them that you are wiling to have fun and open up, they are willing to give back the same. I was in a job prior to joining Yamaha and my boss there stood back and watched us work. He didn't create a fun environment; he didn't roll up his sleeves and help out. He seemed aloof, so I didn't feel like I could go to him. I did not want to go that direction as a manager."

To attract and retain the best people, employees need to feel a supervisor's personal interest, have their opinions matter, and feel integral to the organization's mission. Again, just a little respect.

NINE-TO-FIVE ADVERSARIES

The atmosphere of *us versus them* is prevalent at too many organizations. It is unfortunate, but employers and their employees often feel an adversarial relationship. Even in organizations that try to be civil and forward thinking, the dynamics of management have an inherent inclination toward dictatorship if left unchecked. Isn't it funny that despite all of the business talk about the importance of teams and cooperation, humorous television shows like *The Office* and newspaper cartoons like *Dilbert* have become such entertainment phenomena? The antics of these bumbling, tyrannical managers still ring true for millions of workers. Organizations are simply not getting the message.

So how best to bridge the divide between employees? The answer is elusive, not because it is difficult, but because it can't be addressed by the rollout of a new program. A catchy aphorism can't replace a systematic change of individual behavior. How do you gain trust? You have to earn it. You have to be fair and generous.

All of which takes us back to levity. Sharing a laugh with someone is an incredibly powerful way to foster trust and rapport. It's also efficient, if you think about it. How much time or effort does it take to share a joke with somebody or let off a little steam with an upbeat activity like playing a round of Nerf darts? It's the best time investment you'll ever make.

And yet so many adults are suspicious of having fun. A recent study of preschool children noted that children laugh up to 400 times a day. What's your guess on the number of laughs adults manage to wedge into their schedules? You're not going to like this: 15 laughs. Ouch! And that's generous for some sourpusses you know, right? No wonder kids think adults are about as fun as a box of hair.

Levity is the link between trust, respect, and the engagement of a workforce. It is human alchemy. When atmospheres of friendship are present at the workplace—the kind of friendship that values diversity, encourages the participation of everyone, acknowledges all contributions, allows people to be personable, lets people find joy in what they do and with whom they do it—then employees will take those qualities of trust and respect and turn them into gold for the organization.

SIDELIGHT
R-E-S-P-E-C-T

10 STEPS TO BUILD A
TRUSTING ENVIRONMENT

Employees are looking for fair treatment. And like the lyrics of the Aretha Franklin song, they are merely asking for, "just a little bit, just a little bit." Here are a few simple suggestions to demonstrate respect for each other at all levels of your organization:

1. Express simple kindness, courtesy, and politeness. Greet people, hold the door for others, mind your Ps and Qs.

2. Be tolerant of people when they make mistakes. Some companies actually pay people when they make mistakes, because it's a lesson learned and useful to the company, and because the employee had the integrity to fess up.

3. Listen first; talk second. Or talk not at all, which in many cases is most appropriate.

4. Stop butting in when others are speaking. You're trying to build trust, not make enemies.

5. Give employees credit when their ideas work. This is the root of most respect and trust issues.

6. Refuse the urge to insult, embarrass, and disparage others. The polar opposites to trust, respect, and encouragement.

7. Involve people in decisions that affect their work lives.

8. Apply the rules to everyone the same way. You may treat people differently with raises and bonuses, but playing favorites with the rules is a quick path to distrust.

9. Let people balance their work lives and home lives.

10. Praise five times more than you criticize. Who would you trust more, someone who continually corrects you or someone who frequently and specifically praises you and only corrects when necessary?

CHAPTER FIVE

Levity Effect— Health

Good for What Ails You

Laughing—while not always a symptom or the outcome of fun at work—can improve your overall health. But the funny thing is, some in the academic community initially aimed to prove that laughing was damaging to the body. In the early 1970s, the historically important decade that endowed the world with such scientific breakthroughs as the pantyhose egg and Pong, Dr. William F. Fry Jr. published scholarly articles saying laughter is hazardous because it elevates the heart rate, makes breathing irregular, and may adversely affect hernias and ulcers. The same could be said for sex, of course ("Oh, Phyllis, my hernia!"), but we digress. Norman Cousins's breakthrough research published in *Anatomy of an Illness* helped put to rest Fry's short-lived and even less-believed theory and made popular the notion that humor is not harmful but healing.

While suffering from ankylosing spondylitis, a painful degenerative disease of the connective tissue, Cousins was almost completely paralyzed and given only a couple of months to live. He checked himself out of the hospital, moved into a hotel, and prescribed for himself a regimen of Marx Brothers' movies and comic books, which actually alleviated some of his pain and allowed him to sleep. Humor accomplished more than simply distracting him from pain, it aided in healing. Cousins's influential book ushered in the holistic health movement and created a community of researchers who look at humor from medical, sociological, and psychological vantage points. Correspondingly, there are now academic journals, conferences, university departments, and research institutes all dedicated to humor. Who'd a thunk it?

The study of humor and its effects even has a name, Gelotology, from the Greek word *gelos* (laughter). And the research shows that a good belly laugh has measurable benefits on the heart, blood sugar, stress levels, circulation, the immune system, and more.

And how about this? A study of 2,015 Norwegians diagnosed with cancer discovered that a great sense of humor cut people's chances of death by a whopping 70 percent compared to those with a poor sense of humor. Okay, so maybe you're not a Norwegian or ever plan to become one. But they do have this figured: Laughter is the best medicine, indeed.

To bring this back to a business discussion, levity has also become a subject of study to address questions of employee stress, which leads to burnout, decreased job satisfaction, and eventually turnover. Levity has also been linked to higher incidences and

levels of productivity, loyalty, cooperation, and problem solving. We mention the science angle of levity
because it is often given short shrift: "He's a good
manager; he's so much fun." "She's great at sales because everybody likes being around her." That's
what we say without looking closely at the causes
and effects. In management strategy, there is a dis-
connect between an act of levity and its effect on
people. General observations like those listed earlier
are helpful because they illustrate that our society
does regard humor as an asset. But to really appreciate the real significance of humor in the workplace,
you need to get a bit scientific.

For example: Why do we laugh at a joke?

Because it's funny. Okay, that's a start, but
there's more. For laughter to occur, there has to be
an understanding that is built on a relationship between the sender and the receiver. This transaction
of communication is essentially the same as in any
conversation, but there are a few structural differences. We all know the function of the punch line,
but a joke can't land unless a foundation of understanding is established first. There must be a setup,
a situation or narrative for the joke that becomes its
landscape. And at the end, there's an element of
surprise.

Essential to finding humor in something is the
emotional connection between sender and receiver.
Key to that is having the feeling of being an insider,
that the recipient *gets* it, that he is one of the gang.
There is a bond formed between the communicators,
even if the receiver is mostly a passive listener. This
is an intense relationship; it's strong enough that the
body's physical reaction to humor is considerable. A
one-minute gut buster laugh, for example, affects the

body as powerfully as ten minutes on a rowing machine, according to a recent study. Now, you won't achieve a sculpted and chiseled physique merely by lying in bed wheezing with laughter watching *Letterman*, but the laughs will certainly do your body more good than watching anything starring Olympia Dukakis, for example.

SHARED MEANING

There is an intimacy in humor, an unspoken bond that seems to say, "I know what you're talking about, and although I can't say it as cleverly as you, I agree with you." That's what we communicate when we laugh at a joke. We are entering into a partnership. Like marriage, only funnier.

Humor scholar William Hampes noted in two influential studies that close interpersonal relationships are forged and strengthened through humor. In addition to reducing stress, humor promotes feelings of comfort, and as a by-product, humor increases empathy. Hampes found that individuals who laugh more tend to have more positive and productive relationships. He also demonstrated a correlation between humor and trust—two dynamics of relationships we are all trying to foster at work . . . and at home.

High-humor individuals, according to his research, are better equipped to earn the trust of another individual, in part because humorous people tend to respond to stress in a different manner than others. It is a character trait we all take for granted and need science to make apparent: Levity helps us handle difficult situations. It is the physical manifestation of *perspective*.

Thematically speaking, jokes are serious business. They spur social change. Throughout history, humor has led to a breakdown of prejudices and hatred. By their nature, jokes are considered funny because they point out commonly felt frustrations, the undeniable hypocrisies of politics, the ubiquitous absurdities of modern life and its ironies, and, most important, they poke holes in people who need a little deflation for their own good. They illuminate the details of our lives in ways that a long verbal diatribe can't. It's no surprise that a political cartoon in a newspaper, for example, is as illuminating and often more memorable than a multipage article or a long speech. Some might think that jokes are simply harmless fun, but a lot of proof suggests otherwise. The insightful quality of good jokes ensures that these quips often become part of the common vernacular. Think of any high-level political figure, and you'll also be able to conjure up some comedian's dead-on (and revealing) characterization.

A comedian (professional or not) may show her ability to deliver a well-timed punch line, but the joke has to resonate with the listener to be effective. A common, but inadvertent faux pas, the tone and delivery of the joke must not be condescending toward the audience. It might be satiric, barbed, even slightly insulting, but your audience won't laugh at it unless they can identify that the sender of the communication is honest and insightful. While humor can make us uncomfortable at times, we still find comfort in something about the exchange of it, although its exact parameters are hazily defined.

Science is only beginning to analyze how our brains decode humor. Canadian scientists presented humor to a group of people, half of whom had a brain injury caused by stroke, tumor, or surgical removal of damaged tissue. Participants of the study whose right anterior frontal lobes were damaged couldn't understand jokes (written or spoken) as readily as the unimpaired participants or participants with brain injuries to other parts of the brain. When shown a cartoon and offered various punch lines, injured participants more often chose the incorrect line. They didn't laugh at the cartoons or jokes. Instead, they demonstrated a preference for slapstick comedy. Their favorite type of humor had illogical endings and pratfalls, such as the routines of the Three Stooges, of whom Neil Simon once wrote, "Moe is 55 years old and pokes his fingers in his brother's eyes."

People with brain damage like the Stooges. Enough said.

The studies are interesting because they illustrate how deeply imbedded humor is in our thought processes. Humor is hardwired into our brains; therefore, to understand how people function best, humor has to be considered a factor in the equation.

You might be thinking, yeah, but what has this got to do with my business and me?

Everything.

A William M. Mercer survey showed a scant 29 percent of employers in the United States encourage humor as part of their culture and only eight percent have a policy of using fun to reduce employee stress. But research at California State University Long Beach showed that people who have fun at work are more creative, more productive, work better with others, and call in sick less often—benefits we are all seeking.

Here's another benefit for you.

HEALTHIER HOMES

Research by Lee Berk, a medical researcher in humor and laughter, shows that a good-natured or mirthful laugh can:

- Increase the immune system's activity. Cut NyQuil and Airborne right out of your monthly budget.

- Decrease stress hormones, which constrict blood vessels and suppress immune activity. Stress, constrict, suppress . . . all bad words, gone.

- Increase the antibody immunoglobulin A, which protects the upper-respiratory tract. We're not sure we like the sound of that particular antibody, especially the "glob" part, but if it helps us not "produce" in the middle of a face-to-face conversation, we'll take it.

"Who wouldn't want that kind of benefit?" said Dr. Berk, assistant professor of family medicine at the University of California Irvine. His study shows that if you're employing or experiencing positive humor, then the whole brain is involved in the experience, not just one side, and also there's more coordination between both sides. "When you utilize humor, it makes you less on edge, lowers your blood pressure and your heart rate, and allows you to think more clearly."

Your biology changes with humor. Stress hormones are lessened and the immune system is optimized, which means positive humor, as opposed to mean-spirited or negative joking, is always beneficial in the workplace. And out of it as well.

Whether you are single, married, or in a long-term relationship, have kids, grandkids, or eleven calico cats and a macaw named Tippy, you have relationships that can be enhanced with levity. Many of us worry an inordinate amount about being liked or being engaging at work, but then we walk through our front door at the end of the day and seem to give up. We're tired from work, cranky about having to listen to the whines of kids, intolerant of the demands of our significant others. When we come home from work, we have to make dinner, clean up, help with homework, get kids in the tub and then to bed, pay bills, watch *American Idol*—the chores never end!

Going home can feel like going to a second job. But it helps to think of it that way. In fact, as we travel home to our respective families each night, we've learned to start gearing up as if we really are going to another job. Sometimes we sit in the garage a minute to take a few deep breaths and recapture a little energy before getting out of the car. When we walk through the door, rather than unload the pressures of the day on our families, we do our best to have broad grins as we jovially announce something along the lines of, "It is true. I have returned!" or, "Hello, my queen," or "Don't all rush to hug me at once because I am, in fact, HOOOOoooommme!" Commit yourself to giving your loved ones the same courtesy, attention, and time that you give to your colleagues. If we are ever to be magnanimous and generous, we believe that our families should be the most deserving recipients.

According to a recent survey from Yankelovich, nearly half of all parents surveyed say they are too tired to play with their young children. Play has lost its place in our lives. But play is essential, especially for youngsters. It helps children develop mental and motor skills; improves their creativity, logic, and problem-solving abilities; and even enhances self-esteem, says Professor Gordon Burghardt of the University of Tennessee in his book *The Genesis of Animal Play.*

But play isn't just for kids. It brings us all together and allows us to put the rest of the world on pause while encouraging us to laugh.

We need that play ourselves. The typical adult now works nine more hours per week than our parents did—that's more than another full day on the job. And when we're not working, we are plugged in and tuned out. The Family Research Council found that the average parent spends only 38.5 minutes per week in meaningful conversation with his or her children. But adults spend up to 35 hours per week watching TV, up to 30 hours online, and, get this: More than half of us admit to being so addicted to portable devices that we'll regularly check e-mail in the bathroom, almost 60 percent check e-mail in bed, and 12 percent admit to checking e-mail in church. This is probably making you want to peek at your PDA right now. Go ahead; we'll give you a second.

It's not too late to bring fun back into our personal lives. In our respective homes, we try to make everyday activities more fun. For example, we tell jokes while washing the dishes, we play board games like clockwork every Monday night at seven, and we walk the dog and try to spot different types of birds. But more on this later.

HEALTHIER CULTURES

Is your workplace ill? Do you sense a sickness permeating the cubicles like a plague or the aroma of sour milk? It's not a seasonal bug or virus. It isn't the dreaded 24-hour flu or a hacking cough. It's worse. Where laughter and humor have withered away, in their place you'll find a team or department that doesn't produce. Why? Their spirits are ailing. They need a little levity to help jump-start their creativity and motivation.

Whether a manager or an employee, people with a healthy sense of humor are almost always better communicators and better team players. As we stated earlier, studies have shown that happy workers are more productive. In fact, a researcher at California State University found that humor helps people concentrate on their work more efficiently because it releases tension. What's more, employees who enjoy interacting with their coworkers aren't as likely to be absent from work—because they don't want to disappoint their colleagues or miss out on any fun. You've probably seen this dynamic in action. Where fun and humor are a part of the work culture, you look forward to being there. The fear of missing out on practical jokes or inside humor is at worst a small incentive to be present.

Think about the benefits of encouraging levity. First, employees show up for work. That's good. But while at work, they feel higher levels of satisfaction and glee (yes, glee), which in turn ratchets up their focus and productivity. All because you've caught the vision of frequent and meaningful levity. The lighter the mood, the easier it is to free up the mind. Unleash creativity. Make discoveries. Contribute with impact.

Kal Mistry, senior vice president of the 10,000-employee Vitas Innovative Hospice Care, said her employees are healthier when they are happy and having fun. "Absolutely. Happiness is key to having a healthy body and a clear and tranquil mind," she said. "To be able to have an environment where employees can have fun with their coworkers affects people physically. Hospice work can be physically and emotionally draining. As we laugh and have fun with each other, we are better able to care for our patients and their families with positive attitudes."

Research conducted by psychologist Dr. Ashton Trice at Mary Baldwin College in Virginia showed that humor also helps us think more clearly. When people feel stalled on important projects, they tend to feel angry or depressed. This negative mood can interfere with subsequent performance. According to Dr. Trice's research, taking time out to laugh can help relieve us of negative feelings and allow us to return to a task or move on to another project unaffected by past defeat.

Another helpful hint is to take a *time-out* now and then. You've probably used the time-out method in rearing your little brats, er, dear children. A time-out serves as a diversion from their undesirable behavior, a chance to reset their thinking and behavior, if you will. You can do the same with a little levity at work. Leave your desk, walk around, laugh with fellow cubicle dwellers (where applicable), watch the latest YouTube video that someone e-mailed you (where allowable), or attempt to retell the latest Cubs joke (where advisable).

So, laughter is good for the soul and body. Lightheartedness sometimes equals longevity. How else do you explain comedian George Burns lasting as long as he did puffing cigars all those years? What was he when he died—170? And Bob Hope (named after the Bob Hope Golf Classic) kept it light well into his late 90s.

Religious leader Gordon B. Hinckley lived to the ripe old age of 97. He was still active, lucid, spunky, and most significantly, used humor and levity in his lectures and teachings until the last few days of his life. Hinckley's trademark humor was one of the qualities that endeared him to more than 13 million faithful, worldwide followers. During one very hot afternoon session of his church's general conference, he and the other attendees suffered while the air conditioning was on the fritz in the old building. Hinckley stood up and addressed the sweaty congregation with a gleam in his eye, "It's warm. We're sorry. But it's not as warm as it's going to get if you don't repent!"

These humorous seniors aren't alone. In fact, there is a proven link between sense of humor and longevity, reports Dr. Sven Svebak, president of the International Society for Humor Studies. Also noted has been a definite anesthetic effect of laughter and an inverse relationship between humor and pain.

Whether you really want to live as long as Phyllis Diller or not, you have to admit that it would be nice for the time being to use levity to eliminate some of the anger, stress, or anxiety you experience personally or in your work environment. It may be as simple as finding a quiet place to laugh on your own or sharing a funny story with one of your coworkers.

Just as Weight Watchers and other diets have you count your daily calories to better your health and fitness, you can up your daily laugh count by keeping in mind a goal. Carry a small notebook or index card for a week, and set an objective. Keep track, and try to increase your laughter quota each week.

You only need to observe children at play to appreciate the relationship between humor and enjoying life. Children will laugh at almost anything. And when you ask them why in the world they're laughing, they may say something like, "She looked at me."

But how does a body benefit from a simple laugh? Well, it's actually not that simple physiologically. It's beautifully complicated. "Humor and its partner laughter," says Steven M. Sultanoff, PhD, "activate physiological systems including the muscular, respiratory, cardiovascular, and skeletal. In fact, we may even lose muscle control, as many of us have, when we laugh so hard that we fall down or wet our pants." (The staining of one's drawers is by far the pinnacle of comic measurement; it may not necessarily boost higher levels of workplace loyalty and success, but it will most certainly become a legendary story to tell for those who witnessed it.) "Laughter has been labeled a jogging and juggling of the internal organs. When we laugh we feel physically better, and after laughter we feel lighter and more relaxed."

Try to remember the times in your life when you've actually lost control of your body and fallen right down on the ground in an aching heap of laughs. Your gut was sore, your face red, your eyes teary. This total laugh-induced loss of motor control happened to Scott in his high school production of *To Kill a Mockingbird*. During the tender final act when Scott's character (Atticus) was delivered the bad news that his client was killed trying to escape prison, the actor playing opposite Scott messed up his lines so badly, so obviously and incredibly badly, that Scott couldn't help laughing out loud. His laughter was so full, rich, and powerful that he fell down on the stage, literally kicking his feet and pounding his fists. Initially shocked, the audience followed suit and screams of laughter filled the auditorium for several minutes. The only person not laughing was the director, who sat mortified amid the howling crowd. Everyone was in tears and nursing sore abdominal muscles. That level of laughter produces a natural high that is sweet to the senses. If you've never had such a moment, you've missed one of the greatest experiences an individual could ever have (the potential damp undies being the only negative).

Mankind has actually known about the beneficial effects of laughter for centuries. In medieval times, the court jester was often summoned to try to lift the monarch out of an angry or melancholic mood. Certainly, there was no shortage of stress in the life of royalty in medieval times (imagine the constant threat of an assassin's arrow from a grassy knoll whilst waving to villagers from an open carriage). Even monarchs understood the magic of mirth in settling their psyches.

SIDELIGHT
HEALTHY HEAD

8 WAYS LAUGHTER STRENGTHENS YOUR SANITY

Levity boosts more than our physical health; it boosts our mental health as well. Here's how:

1. Levity helps us connect with others. By acting as a social lubricant, laughter gets us all

greasy and slimy . . . and helps us loosen up. It's a lot easier to talk with others when you feel at ease.

2. Levity helps us get rid of bad feelings. You cannot feel angry, depressed, anxious, guilty, or resentful and experience humor at the same time. It's like trying to enjoy a glass of orange juice after brushing your teeth; it's just not going to happen. Lacking humor will cause your thought processes to stagnate, leading to increased distress. The more you allow humor to rattle around your head, the more freed up your thoughts become. Jaw clenching restricts your ability to generate good ideas.

3. Levity can yank us out of our antisocial shells. When we experience humor, we talk more, make more eye contact with others, touch people more (in appropriate ways), and so on.

4. Levity gives us passion. With increased energy, we may perform activities that we might otherwise avoid, and we get more done in a shorter amount of time.

5. Levity just makes us feel great!

Easier said than done? Here are some specific ways in which to use laughter to improve your mood and overall enjoyment of life:

6. Laugh things off instead of complaining about them. You've certainly been around someone who has nothing positive to say about

anything. They punctuate each conversation with thoughts such as, "I hate Mondays," "This job sucks," or "I've been probed by aliens." Do you like to be around that person? Does anyone? Are you that person? To quote *Monty Python's Life of Brian*, "Always look on the bright side of life." Laugh. Smile. Giggle. No matter how stressful work may be, it's time to incorporate more humor.

7. **Laugh to get rid of frustrations.** In ancient times, the court jester's job was to diffuse tense situations, even imminent battles, by acting the fool. The combatants on both sides would get caught up in laughter and become distracted. The harder they cackled, the more they released angry emotions harmlessly. While sharing a good laugh together the lust for fighting would wane. Both parties would agree to disagree and be done with it. (Sure, eventually they would disembowel one another, but what are you going to do?)

8. **Laugh when you're nervous.** We've all heard the advice about visualizing your audience in their underwear if you're nervous about giving a public speech. Believe it or not, this technique can work. Just be careful about whom you're envisioning in their skivvies. You may end up with a faster heartbeat and sweatier palms than you started with. Whatever gives you mental anxiety, meet it head on in your mind and then think about it a little left of center.

CHAPTER SIX

Levity Effect— Wealth

Laughing All the Way to the Bank

If you're looking for a levity-filled, laugh-a-minute place to work, chances are excellent that one of the Big Four accounting firms would not be high on your list of prospects. In fact, they probably wouldn't make your list at all. Or anyone's for that matter. Historically, accounting firms have pretty much defined the antithesis of fun.

But what if, suddenly, an accounting giant chose to apply the Levity Effect and inject regular fun initiatives into its work routine?

That's exactly what happened at KPMG. This Big Four accounting firm has made a concerted effort over the last several years to turn itself into an Employer of Choice (EOC) by increasing its focus on people-centric programs and initiatives. The comprehensive effort,

which has included the introduction of myriad initiatives to help employees develop satisfying careers
while balancing the responsibilities of work and their
personal lives, made the firm's EOC aspirations a reality, evidenced by the fact that employee survey ratings
on the statement, "Taking everything into account,
this is a great place to work," increased 23 points
since the introduction of EOC.

But even with this drastic upswing in employee
ratings, KPMG leadership knew they couldn't rest on
their laurels, because being an EOC takes an ongoing commitment. And while reviewing employee survey results, they were surprised to discover that two
of the top five predictors of positive employee responses to the critical "great place to work" question
were, "We are a close-knit team or family," and "I
have fun at work."

KPMG's leaders decided they couldn't argue with
the numbers—especially because they're hard-core
number crunchers at heart. So in early 2007, the
firm introduced a new "Esprit de Corps" initiative as
part of its ongoing Employer of Choice efforts. The
program's main objectives are to thank employees
for their hard work and commitment, celebrate successes, and bring some fun and camaraderie into the
workplace. The first initiative was a "Movie Madness
Challenge" that encouraged employees to go to the
company's intranet to choose Oscar winners. Those
who tallied the most correct choices were entered
into a drawing for prizes that included plasma TVs,
portable DVD players, iPods, and free movie tickets.
The results were convincing, even for the critics.

"When we introduced the movie challenge, some
leaders asked, 'Who is going to do this? Our people

are too busy.'" admitted Bruce Pfau, KPMG's vice chair of Human Resources. "More than 10,000 of our 22,000 employees logged in to participate during a very busy season when it's difficult just to get the attention of our people. It said to me, 'Our accountants and auditors are hungry for some fun.'"

Encouraged by the results, leadership has continued to sponsor fun initiatives. For instance, when the firm surprised its employees with an unexpected five-day weekend for the Fourth of July, leadership wanted to drive home the message that people should make the most of the extra time off. So they mailed gift certificates to every employee's home for a free "Barbecue Bonanza" package from Omaha Steaks that included four steaks, eight hamburgers, eight hot dogs, and eight chicken breasts. Then there was the "National Vacation Challenge" that invited people to upload their best vacation photos for the chance to win prizes. Partners and employees submitted almost 7,000 photos, and winners were selected by their peers at both local and national levels to receive travel vouchers that they could use when planning their next vacations. Hit counts show that a majority of employees went online to vote and, likely, laugh at the images. More recently was a "World Series Challenge" contest in which employees competed for prizes that included a grand prize, all-expenses-paid trip for two to New York City to attend Major League Baseball's All-Star Week festivities, as well as video game consoles and baseball jerseys.

Scores on the most recent employee survey have continued to climb, and the positive momentum has helped earn the firm a spot on *Fortune*'s "100 Best Companies to Work For," as well as in the top ten of

Working Mother's "100 Best Companies" list, and on *BusinessWeek's* "50 Best Places to Launch a Career."

In addition, KPMG's annualized employee turnover is at historic lows for the organization, which according to *BusinessWeek* has the best three-year retention rate for entry-level hires among the Big Four accounting firms.

Like KPMG, companies that create the Levity Effect at work experience higher productivity, engagement, and retention. For individual leaders, the financial rewards hit even closer to home: Leading with levity is proven to increase upward mobility and salary levels. Let's talk turnover first.

LEVITY LOWERS TURNOVER

The cost of replacing one employee has been estimated at anywhere from a few thousand dollars to up to three times the previous worker's salary. So it's no surprise that just about every leader we talk to tells us retention of valuable employees is a critical issue for their firm. Research shows that up to 3 in 10 workers don't feel committed to their organizations and don't plan to stay for more than a couple years.

In the restaurant business, where turnover can commonly run up to 300 percent per year, attrition—which can quickly swallow up an already slim profit margin—is a particular concern. Fortunately, Boston Pizza International has discovered that a healthy dose of fun does wonders to retain employees—even in their toughest markets.

"It's proven time and again in our internal research, the franchises with the highest overall department satisfaction and the lowest turnover scores are the ones that respect their people; they have a great, fun time together; and there's a sense of camaraderie and teamwork," said Caroline Schein, vice president of People Development.

Research by Dr. David Abramis at California State University Long Beach validates the restaurant chain's findings. During a trial period where humor was incorporated into the workplace of the studied environments, turnover fell by 21 percent and absenteeism dropped by 38 percent.

To Schein, the connection is a no-brainer. "As an employee, if I have a choice and I can choose two companies, but at one I feel welcome, have fun, and feel a sense of belonging, why would I leave, even if I know I can make a bit more money elsewhere? Money is what gets people in the door initially, but it's not what keeps them. It's the environment, the teamwork, and the ability to have fun."

All of that is summed up in the company's internal and external tag line: "You're among friends."

"It's a fact that to be an Employer of Choice, to hang on to good people—and I've done many focus groups and surveys on this—our employees want to work with their friends. So you have to find that balance where you are being productive and getting your work done, but you create an environment where they are having fun with their friends."

It's finding that balance that most leaders worry about. How convinced are you that putting "friends together that are having fun" won't turn into a time and productivity black hole? The balance is not always easy, but for those companies that get it right, it is lucrative. Research from the Great Place to Work® Institute found that employees who considered their supervisor a friend were more likely to experience high job satisfaction than those who didn't (54 percent to 30 percent) and were much less likely to look for another job in the next two years (28 percent to 45 percent). And, as we know, satisfaction and retention affect the bottom line.

Knowing this, Boston Pizza brings in the new management team before every franchise opens. In addition to food prep and accounting, trainers actually help managers learn how to have fun with their staff members—something unheard of within most industries.

A recent study by William M. Mercer found that 63 percent of company executives were either neutral on the topic or had never thought about humor. Only 8 percent reported that they include fun as part of their values or mission statement, while another 8 percent said that they actively *discourage* the use of humor in the workplace.

"We sing songs, dance, and encourage the management team to start leading the fun because we know it will help retain great employees," said Schein. "We can't mandate what our franchises do, but we see that the high-performing restaurants that have the lower turnover, where you just walk in and feel the great team environment, they're the ones that have team contests, dress-up days tied in with the menu promotions, and they are always cracking jokes."

LEVITY RECHARGES BATTERIES

Art Hargate isn't a basketball player, but in his job as CEO of Ross Environmental Services, he thinks like one.

"Good athletes know that when they train, they stress their bodies, and they also know that they can't do it continuously or they'll break down," he explains. "It's the same thing in business. So yeah, you work hard, but then you have to back off. You have to relax and let the work muscles rebuild."

According to Hargate, on one hand, taking a fun breather allows employees to approach work with renewed energy and passion. Keeping them on a continuous full-court press, on the other hand, exhausts their enthusiasm for the job.

"When you walk up to an employee and say, 'There's a lot of work out there. I've got a bunch more work for you,' his response is going to go one of two directions. Either it will be, 'Oh (swell), more work? I don't want more work!' Or it will be, 'Great. Bring it on.' The difference is whether he's had time to rejuvenate."

At Ross Environmental Services, fun has measurably increased employee productivity. Since consciously incorporating levity into the workplace in 2004, the company has achieved 7 to 8 percent annual growth.

"Having a sense of humor and allowing people to be human has certainly contributed to our success," says Hargate. "I think we're in a better position to respond to the demands of a busy market, ready to say, 'Bring it on,' because we're learning how to relax more."

A growing body of research supports the claim that humor increases productive work behaviors. Here are just two examples:

1. Twenty middle managers at Digital Equipment Corporation in Colorado Springs, Colorado,

increased their productivity by 15 percent and reduced their sick days by half in the nine months following a humorous workshop designed to help them loosen up.

2. Research has shown that a 13 percent increase in morale can result in a 40 percent increase in productivity.

The Levity Effect consistently triggers these kinds of results around the world, within different companies and cultures. It doesn't matter how a leader goes about it, as long as she is making efforts to increase fun at work, energy, and morale.

At Nike, for instance, the unwritten law of "work hard, play hard" is expressed in small but significant ways, says Dave Clark, vice president of Human Resources. "This is a small example, a day-to-day example, but we really want people to have fun at work, so we allow people to have coolers at their work stations. And at the end of the day, if you want a beer, you have at it. We don't have HR or Security walking around emptying the coolers."

Lisa Martini, public relations manager at Enterprise Rent-A-Car, sees fun expressed in the relaxed interplay between employees. "We absolutely do laugh a lot. It's just something that happens. We're telling stories and playing off each other or the material we're working on. It's not planned; it's of the moment."

Rather than discouraging the levity, Enterprise leadership understands that lighthearted moments like these are part of what makes their organization great.

"If you were to look at some of our top branches you'd find that they don't take themselves seriously all the time. They have fun together," said Martini.

The effects of levity on productivity are even illustrated a world away at the Sierra Leone office of Victor Angelo, U.N. executive representative of the Secretary General. There, the culture is such that many employees will have as many as 20 to 25 relatives dependent on a single salary. And that kind of pressure is intense. So Angelo works very hard to create an environment where employees can enjoy themselves.

"We make sure the workplace is very different from employee homes. It's comfortable. If they want to stay late and watch TV and movies, they can. You create an environment in the office that shows it's possible to live well and know that we care about them."

In the beginning, Angelo recalls, his colleagues were worried that people would be distracted by having a little fun. Their concerns turned out to be unfounded. "We've seen an increase in productivity, and employees are always willing to stay longer hours if we need them," said Angelo. "There is a commitment that comes from managing in this way."

HUMOR INCREASES
PERSONAL SUCCESS

Research by the Federal Reserve Bank of St. Louis found that good-looking, slim, tall people tend to make more money than the rest of us (Danny DeVito being the obvious exception). Now, if that were the only factor that determined success, most of us would be flat out of luck. Fortunately, it's not. In September 2003, the *Harvard Business Review* reported that executives with a sense of humor climb the corporate ladder more quickly and earn more money than their counterparts. So you can either grow taller and better looking or bone up on a few jokes.

Scott's father, Jim (only 5′9″ and no George Clooney), was hired on by Busch Gardens Florida amusement park a few years ago to keep himself occupied in his retirement and make a little extra pocket money. Jim was assigned to be the tour guide on the Serengeti Express, the little train that winds its way around the park passing by a variety of zoo animals. It didn't take long for "Conductor Jim" to carve his own niche as a memorable and engaging guide.

"They gave me about an 18-page script that I had to memorize and recite each trip. I asked them if I could, you know, add some of my own stuff to it," Jim said. "They looked baffled. 'What do you mean—add stuff?' they asked. I just wanted to liven it up a bit and give 'em a little more bang for their buck. They said as long as I covered the scripted parts then it would be okay."

Jim began adding his own commentary, jokes, animal impressions, and songs. Soon the queue at the train station got longer and longer as word got out that the old fellow running the show was a hoot. "How refreshing," they'd say.

Conductor Jim started to receive commendations from the park guests. Commendations are a way for park employees to earn bonus pay. For each note of praise received, an employee gets a $10 spiff. Jim had asked the HR folks what the empty bulletin board in the break room was for. They told him it was designed to pin up the commendations, but that nobody ever received one. So Jim set out to get some. In just a few weeks, Jim earned 45; and when August Busch the company president visited the park, he asked to meet the amazing Conductor Jim. A little levity paid off.

As it does at all levels. In fact, funny executives perform better. No one knows this better than Fabio Sala at the Hay Group's McClelland Center for Research and Innovation. He has conducted several studies on executives deemed "outstanding" by their bosses and those termed "average." The executives were all interviewed by Sala to determine the number of "humor utterances," and he coded the humor as negative, positive, or neutral. Humor was negative if it was a put-down to someone, positive if used to politely disagree, and neutral if used simply to point out something funny or absurd.

The executives who had been ranked as outstanding used humor more than twice as often as the average, and most of their humor was positive or neutral.

But here's where it gets really interesting for all of us, the money angle. As Sala looked at compensation for the year, he found that the size of the executives' bonuses was correlated positively with their use of humor. In other words, the funnier the executive, the bigger the bonus.

How could being humorous translate into personal business success? For one reason, levity leaders look for fun in the most unlikely places. Take the example of Sir Richard Branson. Two decades ago he had an interesting idea: Entertainment could revolutionize the airline business. He invested in an industry that treated its customers poorly and decided to loosen it up and give them a fun experience. Critics scoffed at the idea. But Virgin flourished, as did its founder's numerous bulging bank accounts.

What Branson understood years ago is just beginning to be embraced by other corporate leaders:

Employees, leaders, and consumers need to let their hair down and have a little fun. In fact, Branson was one of the first to pioneer seatback videos so customers could pick their own movies, instead of being subjected to *Benji Reborn.* He recalls the cost of investing in the new seatback entertainment centers was around $8 million, and the airline was quite stretched at the time. He said, "I went to the bank, and they wouldn't give us the money. So I rang up the head of Boeing and said that we wanted to order some new 747s and could he give us seatback videos, and he said yes. We were able to borrow $2 billion to buy a new fleet of planes, but not $8 million for seatback videos."

While the bank didn't exactly catch the vision of fun, levity helped separate Branson's Virgin brand from a sky full of mediocrity.

HUMOR MAKES YOU EMPLOYABLE

A decade ago, Adrian was interviewing for an executive-level position at a 30,000-person firm. He had read the annual report . . . twice . . . talked to experts in the industry, bought a new dark blue suit, and was by far the most prepared person applying. Indeed he sailed through the first rounds of interviews and impressed the CEO in a one on one with his knowledge of their business. The last hurdle was to meet with the senior executive team, his soon-to-be colleagues. More of a formality, really.

They were a pleasant bunch. They even tried to distract him from the business at hand by tossing him a few softballs of lightness to see how he would react. But Adrian was all business. He shrugged off the silliness and answered questions with earnest sincerity. After all, this was a very large organization in a very serious business. They didn't want a goofball working alongside them.

Whoops. Yes they did. The team had already gauged his qualifications from his curriculum vitae. Now they wanted to know if they could work with this guy every day for the next twenty years.

He didn't get the job. The debrief from the head of the hiring committee was telling. The fellow who got the job was "the person you'd most want to go to a party with."

Indeed, as the neophyte humorist learned, coming across as affable and easy to work with is as important as your qualifications.

"I think the people that get hired and move up the ladder quickest here at Enterprise are the ones that have great interpersonal skills," said Nina McVey, assistant vice president at the rental car company.

Among many in upper management, like McVey, humor is viewed as an outward expression of inner competencies. Not long ago, a survey of vice presidents and directors showed that 84 percent felt that employees with a sense of humor were more effective. The survey concluded: "People with a sense of humor tend to be more creative, less rigid, and more willing to consider and embrace new ideas and methods."

And they may be right. Research also shows that *transformational leaders*—leaders who promote the highest levels of individual and organizational performance—are shown to use humor more often than their less-effective counterparts.

Humor also demonstrates a greater emotional maturity. While great leaders certainly project an image of seriousness, at the same time they demonstrate an ability to laugh at themselves.

They are the types who will catch the eye of a CEO, like Jim Olson, president of Harman Management. "I want a positive, upbeat person on the job because that brings more energy that passes on to me, and I pass it on to other people," says Olson. "So I like to surround myself with what I call 'big personalities.' And that includes outgoing, positive people who are able to engage other people. People who can have fun."

Indeed, there is a growing movement of the converted who are convinced that the only reason one of us (Scott) actually has a job is because of his sense of humor and impetuous playfulness. (It certainly can't be his qualifications or resume.)

Once understood, the link between humor and improved financial returns can be intoxicating, if not sobering. When leaders first hear about the wealth born of the fun movement, visions of new Hummers and endless business golfing fill their heads faster than you can say "heated marble toilet seat." That is, until they realize that fun might cost a little money.

Many business leaders remain unwilling to make even a small investment in fun, which strikes Jim Olson as silly. "If you look at it from a business standpoint, fun reduces turnover, gets people more engaged in the work, and increases productivity. It just makes good business sense."

At Enterprise, every branch has a budget, a dollar amount for employee fun whether that's an employee picnic or party or however they want to celebrate. Fun is a line item in the budget.

McVey laughs when we mention that other leaders have difficulty making that commitment. "I know a

lot of leaders say, 'We don't have money for
Well, we make sure we have money for it because we
know it absolutely pays off."

And indeed by now we hope you are converted too—
realizing that levity pays off in many ways. The second
part of this book, or what we've ingeniously dubbed
Part II, discusses *how* you can lighten up the office
culture, your presentations, and your personal life.

SideLight
Fun 2.0

6 Ways Techno-Levity Can Help You
Reach a New Generation

It's a brave new world, and there are twenty-first-
century ways to have fun using your corporate intranet. Many of these will help you reach your
Generation Y or Millennial employees, most of whom
ignore memos but read anything electronic:

1. *Create a social media site:* Several progressive
   companies we visited have started their own
   Facebook-style sites, exclusively for internal
   employees. People can share information on
   themselves, including a picture or two, but
   they can also pose and answer work-related
   questions, share stories and customer experiences, even crack a joke: "Two baby boomers
   are test-driving Buicks. . . ."

2. *Post fun news:* Smart organizations ensure
   everything and anything possibly entertaining is posted and easy to find online, from
   company softball schedules to bowling league

news, from chili cook-offs to pending parties. Zappos.com promotes its annual head-shaving and beard-growing contests via their intranet.

3. *Coach online:* E-learning and personalized instruction can be effective via technology but only if they are fun and interactive. Two quick rules: (1) keep learning modules to under 10 minutes, and (2) make sure there are fun quizzes and graphics.

4. *Make it personal:* List birthdays, anniversaries, changes in work assignments, and so on. And let employees post information they feel is important—from movie reviews to the weather forecast.

5. *Have contests:* Every now and then have employees participate in a contest with prizes for the winners. KPMG had contests to pick the Oscar winners and download crazy vacation photos, and thousands of their employees logged on to participate and lighten up a stressful business.

6. *Make 'em laugh when they log on:* Make it fun to access your intranet. Try a Face Recognition Game, for example, giving employees a multiple choice of names next to the picture of the employee who pops up. It's a great way to familiarize people with others in the company and create more of a family atmosphere.

PART II

GETTING LIGHTER

Many companies organize fun one-day retreats playing golf or bring in amusing speakers for an afternoon, but come next business day, it's back to grim business. All the momentum born of their well-intentioned levity goes buh-bye. How do great organizations bring a structured and sustained sense of fun to the workplace?

In the following chapters, we'll provide some creative strategies to help businesspeople and organizations use the Levity Effect every day, including hundreds of practical ideas you can use tomorrow. We'll answer the common objections you'll face in having fun. We'll show you some case studies of great fun cultures from the Great Place to Work research. We'll help you apply the Levity Effect in all areas of your life. And finally, we'll discuss the Time-and-Place Rule and sustaining the Levity Effect.

First, over the next few pages, we present the basic blueprint that many organizations follow to build a culture that encourages consistent fun throughout the year. Your goal: levity that never loses steam.

- *Build from respect.* If you work harder to create a positive, courteous, trusting environment, people will naturally start to loosen up. Spend time teaching managers to listen to their employees, to be more open in their communication styles, and to be more deferential of employee opinions.

- *Have employee champions.* It may sound trite to have a Fun Bunch, but the best organizations we've studied have a person or rotating employee team that worries about creating fun activities on a regular basis. If it's assigned, it'll get done. And if employees complain about how cheesy an activity is, then ask them to be part of the team.

- *Get senior management buy-in.* With the research backing this idea and with the common sense most leaders are born with, your management team should buy into the need to build a stronger culture through some fun team-building activities. Get leaders on board piecemeal, and then shower them with success stories at every step along the way.

- *Link fun to work.* Fun work-related contests will help drive sales. Humor can make your customer presentations more effective. Fun will help you brainstorm and be innovative. Fun celebrations of work successes will build camaraderie. At least once a month, you should be doing something fun that is directed at helping your organization grow.

- *Keep it personal.* Onboard new employees into a fun, engaging culture from the first day (we explain this more in Chapter 8). Celebrate individual birthdays (not in the convenient, impersonal once-a-month catchall). Have fun during the December holidays, at Halloween, on Arbor Day, and so on. Start a tradition of acknowledging the happiest person of the week in each staff meeting.

- *Recognize, recognize, recognize.* Cultures that are effective at recognizing excellence are up to three times more profitable than their competitors. Recognition and rewards are fun by their nature. Develop and implement a plan to recognize individuals and teams, and you'll not only have built-in excuses for fun, but you'll spur great achievements.

- *Be consistent.* Make fun an unfailing part of who you are as an organization. Every day, take a moment to make a customer or employee laugh, take a break and throw the Frisbee, play some great music way too loud in the afternoon, create a fun traveling award, take an afternoon off to visit the zoo. Whatever works in your culture, make it genuine and real, and it will keep going and going.

SIDELIGHT
HAVING FUN YET?

AT THESE COMPANIES, THE ANSWER
IS A RESOUNDING . . . DUH!

Storage is the Container Store's specialty. Shelves, boxes, cabinets, chests—you name it; they've got it. But there's one thing the Container Store can't contain—their levity. It just keeps popping up all over.

During the 2007 "100 Best Companies to Work For" selection process conducted by the Great Place to Work® Institute, more than 90 percent of employees at the Container Store indicated that often or almost always "This is a fun place to work." Nine other companies achieved similar results, ranking as the top 10 most fun places to work.

Want to know who they are? Your wish is our command:

1. Container Store (2,866 employees)
2. W. L. Gore & Associates, Inc. (4,945 employees)
3. Standard Pacific (2,856 employees)
4. Starbucks (109,873 employees)
5. Recreational Equipment, Inc. (REI) (8,522 employees)
6. Quicken Loans (3,512 employees)
7. Google (5,063 employees)
8. Nugget Market (1,099 employees)
9. David Weekley Homes (1,622 employees)
10. Bain & Company (1,370 employees)

Looking at this list, it's hard not to notice the variety. There are big and small companies and organizations in industries from finance to professional services, from high tech to construction, and from sporting goods to food services.

The common denominator is fun. And you can create that anywhere. (Even at the place *you* work.)

CHAPTER SEVEN

142 Ways to Have Fun at Work

How to Bring the Levity Effect to Work

Over the next few pages, you'll find myriad ways to start bringing levity into the workplace. Remember levity is, as Monty Python defined it, "the opposite of gravity." It's about lightening up and allowing others to do the same. Where humor and mirth grow organically, born spontaneously from trusting relationships, these suggestions may be unnecessary. But in our experience, the wheels must be set in motion with some committed attempts at *programmed* fun.

Don't reject the list if a few seem out of character for your organization. Move on and find something that will work. And don't quit if you try one and it fails. Just try something else, all the while continuing to show your people that you're committed to building a workplace where trust, respect, friendship, and camaraderie are indispensable.

Here then, in no particular order, are 142 ways to apply the Levity Effect at work. Every single idea listed here was supplied to us by actual people in actual organizations who are actually trying to (pause for dramatic effect) live the dream. We begin:

1. Play work bingo by filling in a square each time your team completes a task or has an achievement. When a manager has signed off on five in a row, the employee or team wins a prize.

2. Offer to shave your head if your team reaches a goal. If you're already bald, offer to paint your dome.

3. Have a tailgate party in the parking lot.

4. Make customers feel like royalty. Dr. Vik at Zappos.com has a throne in his office, along with a selection of crowns and tiaras, and snaps two Polaroid pictures of every visitor, employee, and vendor. One picture is attached to the company's wall of fame; the other is taken home by the person in the photo to remind them that they are royalty at Zappos.com and that they are the king, queen, prince, or princess in their own lives.

5. Hold a quarterly potluck lunch with some kind of fun theme. The folks at the Missouri Department of Transportation charge $3 and make sure all the proceeds go to a local charity.

6. *From the minds at Whole Foods Market (No. 5 on the "100 Best Companies to Work For"*

list, 2007): Paint a break room wall with chalkboard paint, allowing employees to express thanks, pass on messages, or doodle to their hearts' content. At Whole Foods, the store team leader even writes her weekly updates on the wall, rather than sending out a memo. Employees read it while eating lunch or taking a break, making their leader and her message more visible and down to earth.

7. On the third Thursday of the month, go to a pub for food and/or drinks and celebrate achievements, anniversaries, and just making it through another month.

8. Plan a float trip together down a local river or creek.

9. On Halloween, invite employees' kids to come to your workplace dressed up so that they can go trick or treating throughout the office. Have special prizes if they dress up like the boss.

10. Have a family ice skating event.

11. Have a family-not-invited Texas hold 'em tourney.

12. Have a retro day where employees dress up in clothes from whatever era they choose. Have great prizes to make sure people actually do it.

13. Have a theme day and have employees decorate their cubicles and compete for prizes.

14. When you reach a goal, have executives prepare breakfast for everyone (nothing says thank-you like crispy bacon).

15. Have a casino night with a sit-down dinner at a casino and $300 in gambling money.

16. On Halloween, invite employees to bring in pumpkins decorated to represent certain management members or famous people.

17. In the summer, bring an ice cream or shaved ice truck onsite.

18. *From the minds at Google (No. 1 on the "100 Best Companies to Work For" list, 2007):* Imbed subliminal messages with the purpose of having everyone in the world use your search engine. No, wait, no need for that. This is more like it: Roller hockey games twice a week in the company parking lot, a baby grand piano in the break room, a Scrabble game that is ongoing throughout the day.

19. To get a meeting started with a bang, have employees come up with two truths about themselves and one lie. Everyone else must guess which one is the lie.

20. Allow for flex time. Letting employees work from home now and then and giving them some flexibility in their schedules shows trust and builds a fun environment.

21. Cari Gray, HR director of Panera Bread, says, "My recruiter and I do a 'hiring dance' every time we get an accepted job offer for a management fill. Whoever is around at the time gets to see it."

22. Have a chili cook-off, with employees bringing their best recipe for prizes.

23. Have a trivia night, including questions about company products and history.

24. Host a bowling event. If your team is too big to take everyone, then each quarter take a few employees for a long lunch and bowling at the alley.

25. On "deadline day" deliver specialty coffee drinks to employees' desks in the morning. Have a pizza lunch. Give out plastic hand-clappers in the afternoon so everyone can "give yourself a hand, you made it through deadline day." Given to us by Debby Kurtz, Monsanto Sales Support Center.

26. Visit a toy store for items to kindle creative thinking in meetings.

27. Halloween dress up is big at Enterprise Rent-A-Car as employees at many branches go all out to create wacky and memorable costumes. It has become a much anticipated event.

28. Set up a mini golf course at the office.

29. Loosen up by having a game afternoon at work. Play games like Nintendo, foosball, board games, and card games.

30. Instead of using the CEO, hire a comedian to emcee your next big event.

31. Have a pool party at the manager's house with a potluck dinner.

32. At a company offsite, get things going with a game of Scattergories or Pictionary that is based on company history or products.

33. Have a barbecue or Dutch oven dinner at your manager's house with silly backyard games such as a three-legged race or lawn darts.

34. Have an April Fools' Day story in your company publication, and encourage a few harmless April Fools' Day jokes around the office.

35. Challenge another department to a softball game at a local park.

36. Have a Customer Name Remembering Contest.

37. Have employees elect a new manager for a day from their ranks. The existing manager does the employee's job for the day.

38. Go see some clean improv comedy together.

39. Invite employees over to watch a sporting event together at the manager's house on a big-screen TV.

40. Have a St. Urho's Day celebration: At Caribou Coffee, one of the nation's largest gourmet coffeehouses, they believe this obscure saint deserves a celebration. Team members celebrate this holiday in honor of St. Urho (who, as you undoubtedly are aware, chased grasshoppers out of ancient Finland) by enjoying grasshopper pie and grape juice. Yummmee.

41. Take the executive team outside and scrub and buff every employee's car until it shines.

42. Have meetings outside or at a local park.

43. Rent a pool hall, and hold a department tourney.

44. Have a joke of the day. Employees and bosses take turns in your daily stand-up meeting telling a joke.

45. *From the minds at Pella (No. 59 on "100 Best Companies to Work For" list, 2007):* Make training into a party. During Engineering Week, employees and their families were invited to enjoy an event at the new Science Center in Des Moines, which included a booth where children were encouraged to try to break a window by hitting a baseball through it. There was a method to the madness: The window was made of hurricane glass, which can break, but will not shatter; and while the children (and grownups) were batting, the employees were learning about the product's advantages.

46. Build a Wall of Fame. Decorate it with pictures of your team members, thank-you notes from clients, and news clippings of your company's success.

47. Start a meeting with the singing of the national anthem, giving a prize to anyone who can sing it without missing a word.

48. Decorate your office with Pez dispensers, Mr. Potato Heads, Barrels of Monkeys, Bobbleheads, and the like.

49. Once every few weeks, send on an appropriate bit of humor received via e-mail.

50. Instead of all day, have a casual day that starts at noon on Wednesday. Have people

bring their casual clothes to change into over the lunch hour.

51. Have a song of the day that blasts out at a set time in the afternoon. Try to make it describe what's going on that day, special events, the mood, current events, or just an upbeat song that fires people up.

52. Bring food from home: we spoke to a group of managers at HMS Host, the company that caters and manages many airport food services and restaurants. One of the managers said that every so often she'll whip up a bunch of spaghetti for her people. They love the spaghetti, and they're thrilled to eat food that isn't something from work.

53. Have a best cookie contest.

54. Cover fun events in your company newsletter—encouraging other areas to lighten up a little.

55. Give out a happiest person award. Employees at Budget Rent A Car in western Canada's corporate office find that August and September are their busiest and most stressful months. So they decided to see who could be the happiest person each week. At the end of each day, employees cast votes. On Friday, the winner found balloons and other prizes at his or her desk. Employees say it helps morale and gets people's mind off the pressure they face.

56. Have a marathon of *The Office* at the office. Gather everyone to watch the best episodes of NBC's hit show during lunch for a week.

57. Buy books for your team and have a book club. Discuss the book each week at a team lunch.

58. Without changing your voice, page yourself over the intercom.

59. Have fun contests and promotions for your customers, and encourage your employees to ham it up.

60. Have one of the leaders dress up like Frosty the Snowman or Santa Claus (most everyone's cool with a pseudo-religious fictional character that gives presents) and deliver holiday bonus checks to each employee while parading around to either seasonal music or something bawdy and burlesque.

61. During sales conferences or other management retreats and meetings, hire an outside speaker to speak on a lighter topic, such as, oh, levity in the workplace. We can't count the times conference attendees have expressed appreciation to the organizers for bringing us in to lighten the mood.

62. Ring a gong when you win a big deal. Professional services and information technology company CACI International Inc. employs a large antique gong for just this purpose, and ringing it to celebrate good news has been a part of CACI's culture since the 1970s. When the company wins a new contract, President and CEO Paul Cofoni invites the winning team to strike the gong during a top management meeting. When the award is a "recompete" victory

with an established customer, the team celebrates with a two-gong ring—the second signifying the continued business win with the client.

63. Buy a pool table. Have ongoing nine-ball tourneys; the games go faster so more people can play. Some of the most creative ideas are born around a billiards table.

64. Take employees on a go-cart outing. It's plain fun, and it can also bring out the aggressive side in your people before a big project.

65. Add fun or humor to your value statement. At Scripps Networks, humor has been a core value for years—helping attract energized, creative employees.

66. *From the minds at Bain & Company (No. 45 on the "100 Best Companies to Work For" list, 2007):* Create a rock band. The Bain Band is a group made up of volunteer crew members who perform at least once a year during company meetings and other events. And while it started out as one band, spin-offs from the original band have cropped up throughout the Bain system in San Francisco, Toronto, Chicago, Dallas, and New York.

67. Have a parade. Think of a theme—such as ugly Hawaiian shirt day—and march around the office to some tunes.

68. Find fun ways to show off your products to customers. To display a new weapons tracking system, Boeing-SVS employees built a display in their lab complete with a railroad

train set, a small village, and bad guys shooting mortars. Armed Forces brass sat at the console of the tracking system, and instead of looking at a drab lab setting, they looked at a realistic, fun backdrop. And Boeing-SVS got the deal.

69. Have the CEO switch places with an employee for a few days and cover the story in your employee newsletter or video.

70. Do something nice for an employee's family. McLean Company, a large logistics and trucking firm, sends something great to spouses when employees have been on the road a long time.

71. Create a fun committee, and rotate membership.

72. Have a karaoke lunch contest with bosses as contestants and employees as judges.

73. For fellow employees who enjoy keeping things light, make up new nicknames for them everyday. "Nice idea, Coco the Monkey" or "Where you going, Starsky?"

74. Start a work rock band. Practice now and then at lunch, and perform vintage songs at a company event.

75. Perform skits to illustrate the importance of the company value statement.

76. Start a work choir, orchestra, or band.

77. Send fun letters to your staff at home. Include your home address and phone number, and ask them for suggestions.

78. Have impromptu rubber-band wars.

79. Do something fun to greet new hires. Put up a poster, have balloons, buy some bagels, and so on.

80. Have a humor bulletin board. Pick a corner of your break room or other back office area to post cartoons, humorous quotes, and pictures.

81. Have an out-of-the-ordinary holiday party. Last year Scripps Networks took all its Knoxville-based employees (location of the cable networks' headquarters) downtown to a renovated historic theater where they watched the holiday release *Christmas with the Kranks.* Employees ate corn dogs and other movie-themed snacks while being entertained by a humorous local newspaper columnist who writes for one of the EW Scripps' newspapers. After the movie, they took over the local outdoor ice-skating rink, and employees were encouraged to explore downtown shops and restaurants.

82. If you have an issue with people being tardy, organize a voluntary Breakfast Bunch. Late arriving employees pay a small fine and the proceeds are used to buy breakfast once a month.

83. At holiday time, have a white elephant game in the office.

84. Have an office pool for college basketball and football championships, but instead of money have the winner receive a traveling trophy. Have a wacky trophy for the loser too.

85. Whenever employees achieve predesignated goals, have them spin the wheel for a reward such as extra time off or something from the company store.

86. *From the minds at Bingham McCutchen (No. 94 on the "100 Best Companies to Work For" list, 2007):* Plan an *Amazing Race.* In an event for Silicon Valley summer associates, four teams of attorneys imitated the reality TV program where pairs of contestants complete tasks in a whirlwind race around the globe. In this case, Bingham McCutchen employees raced around Palo Alto, California. The contest began with lawyers puncturing balloons with screwdrivers to obtain their instructions, which led them through IKEA, the Stanford Rose Garden, along with other locales. Activities can be work related . . . or not. Either way, it's huge fun.

87. Bring in pizza for lunch.

88. On Fridays, if an employee arrives at work before her manager, she gets to park in his or her reserved parking space.

89. Have a shoes optional day.

90. Have people name their plants. Give them personalities and have others care for them when you are out of the office. Who could forget to water a plant named Steven?

91. Create a break room that really gives employees a break. Include Ping-Pong or foosball tables, board games, art supplies, fun videos, comfy (and clean!) couches, and

lighthearted magazines. Consider holding optional lunchtime activities, like a foosball tournament.

92. Create a miniature golf course out of office furniture and supplies.

93. Have backward races around the office on your chairs.

94. Sing *We Are the Champions* together before a meeting.

95. Have a bring-your-kids-to-work day. Take the youngsters on a tour of the building while various parents talk to the group about their job responsibilities. Hint: If you have bubble wrap in the shipping room, let the kids pop to their hearts' content at the end of the tour.

96. Send 100 roses to someone. There are inexpensive web sites that offer this service.

97. Organize office Olympic events using swivel chairs and other equipment. Solicit volunteers for synchronized swivel chair dancing.

98. Watch a Friday afternoon DVD in the conference room after a week of hard work.

99. Have a family night out. Invite employees and their families to a barbecue, an amusement park, or a semi-pro ball game. Invite spouses, partners, and all the kids and grandkids.

100. Think of creative ways for applicants to submit their work histories.

101. *From the minds at Bright Horizons (No. 92 on the "100 Best Companies to Work For" list, 2007):* There's Mother's Day and Father's Day and Valentine's Day, but what about a special day for the people you spend more time with than the ones at home? Host an employee appreciation day, week, or month each year to show employees that you care.

102. Adopt a funny group mascot, and work together to create silly videos featuring it. We've seen companies employ stuffed monkeys, rubber chickens, and even a G.I. Joe doll. Show the videos each month at staff meetings.

103. Create a funny new employee orientation video.

104. Change hours in the summer. Nike has a Summer Hours initiative where employees are encouraged to finish their work by noon on Friday so that they can leave early. The initiative runs from Memorial Day to Labor Day.

105. Bring in a gorgeous flower bouquet. Each hour of the day, move it to a different employee's desk. At the end of the day, hold a drawing to determine who gets to take it home.

106. Buy people lava lamps as holiday gifts.

107. Have an annual golf outing. Take everyone— the hard-core players and those who've never swung a club—and make it a best-ball scramble.

108. In summer, have a department water-gun fight in the parking lot or a Nerf-gun fight around the desks.

109. Make product quizzes fun with fun prizes.

110. Create a system that brings up a different employee's baby picture at log in, which requires that employees pass a multiple choice guessing game before they can log on to the company intranet.

111. For a gag, take a screen shot of a coworker's desktop and make it the wallpaper image, then drag all the icons off the screen. Just be sure to help them fix it right away.

112. Tack a day onto a business trip to visit a museum, ball game, or something you would consider a pleasurable diversion.

113. Create a yearbook for your team with pictures and stories of accomplishments during the year.

114. Buy the team a cup of coffee or other morning beverage on the way to work.

115. For your next company meeting, have the management team do an *American Idol* or *Dancing with the Stars* skit—just for kicks. Caribou Coffee held its first-ever 'Bou Idol singing contest in 2006 to add fun and excitement to meetings. To enter, a store manager had to call into a dedicated telephone line and sing "Joyful CariBouLand" ("Winter Wonderland" using Caribou Coffee Lyrics). Four winners were selected, and they each sang on stage during the regional fall conferences.

116. Have a human bowling tournament. Strap volunteers to skateboards and push them toward Skittle candies lined up at the end of the parking lot. Tally how many they squish for their score.

117. Race remote control cars around a course marked by orange cones.

118. Quit spending so much time with your low-performing employees and more time with your best. You'll keep the top people and create a more positive work environment.

119. Bring in a masseuse monthly to offer neck and shoulder massages.

120. Starting at five PM, get together to play Halo, Unreal, or another popular computer game.

121. Hunt together. Vitas Innovative Hospice Care has special team-building events where they go offsite for scavenger hunts and other activities to grow closer as a team, let off some steam, and laugh. Overall, Vitas provides a caring and nurturing environment for its employees where appreciation and recognition are celebrated throughout the organization.

122. *From the minds at Bain & Company (No. 45 on the "100 Best Companies to Work For" list, 2007):* The annual Bain World Cup Soccer Tournament played among teams from Bain offices around the world. More than 400 Bain employees participate every year as members of local or regional teams face off to be recognized as the Global Champions.

123. Work together to paint a mural on an office wall, or create some other kind of art together.

124. Have a monthly breakfast meeting. Gather in a new restaurant each time.

125. On a Friday afternoon break, buy cookies, and get everyone together to make a top-ten list of the funniest things that happened at the office that week. (Knowing you have to put together the list usually helps promote more fun.)

126. Give employees their birthdays off with pay.

127. Instead of giving sports tickets to one employee at a time, rent the whole box for a night and take the team and their significant others to a local sporting event. Spring for dinner at the game.

128. Inject some levity into your trainings to keep people alert and focused on the material.

129. Let people leave early once in a while.

130. Take candid photos of employees during work and at company events. Use them during internal PowerPoint presentations to liven things up. Drop in a caption or two if you can.

131. To keep an audience rapt during a presentation, add something humorous every six minutes.

132. Have a take-your-dog-to-work day, a take-your-fish-to-work day, or other pet-related frivolity.

133. Hold meetings away from your traditional conference room.

134. Have everyone try to use—in context—a new, difficult word during the course of a meeting.

135. Play hockey in the hallway.

136. At a meeting, give everyone a funny pen, maybe with a troll or other novelty attached. Without announcing the contest, give a prize to the people who are still writing with the toy attached an hour later.

137. Make your next new hire a comic. Bring in an employee who is naturally funny or has some comedic training.

138. Stop work once a day for your team to give someone a well-deserved standing ovation.

139. Put a piece of exercise equipment—a balance beam works nicely—in the path of the copy machine or the restroom.

140. Sponsor a paper airplane flying contest. Award prizes for distance, style, and trim.

141. Sponsor a seasonal desk- or cube-decorating contest.

142. Incorporate humor into your next print, radio, or TV ad campaign. Make 'em laugh, and they're more likely to remember your product.

CHAPTER EIGHT

Overcoming Objections to Levity

So What if I'm a Brow Knitter?

While the case for personal and organizational levity is compelling, many people still think that lightening up won't work in their environment for one reason or another. What follows are the most common objections we hear when we train and consult on this topic. We've also provided answers based on our experience, the latest research, and input from our interviews:

- *My company tried to have some fun, but they really missed the mark. Employees were rolling their eyes instead of laughing.*

Many company leaders have heard of the use of fun in company success stories—Google, Nike, Southwest

171

Airlines, and others—and have experimented with it themselves, only to summarily abandon it. But fun wasn't the mistake. The problem was the way these company executives approached levity. What's at the heart of these *fun* foibles? First, they didn't understand that laughter is a co-product of trust, which is built from respect. In trusting environments, people can let their hair down. In low-trust environments, no one is going to laugh at the CEO in an Elvis wig or appreciate being herded together to attend the mandatory birthday party for the senior vice president of marketing.

"Fun can't be forced," says Amy Lyman, chair of the Great Place to Work® Institute. "Some organizations try to make the event happen; require people to go to the company picnic, the amusement park, or the ice cream social down the hall. If you are required to go versus you want to go, the event can backfire.

"Genuineness has to come before the fun. In organizations where people have a tremendous amount of fun, it is because it is based on a solid relationship built on trust. The fun activities are similar to those tried at other organizations, yet because there is this base of genuineness in the quality of the relationships, the fun is genuine too. People can choose to participate and want to participate because their friends are there and they feel, 'I'm part of this company, part of this team.'"

So how do you get started building respect and trust? Go back and reread Chapter 4 if you need to. And when you are ready to have fun, start modestly. Many companies link their first fun events to work-related celebrations as a way to acknowledge that this is a workplace, but it's a fun place. Concludes

Lyman, "That connection to work is something we see at the best companies, and it reflects the genuine nature of their fun. Other companies don't always get that."

Indeed, a simple way to enhance camaraderie is to begin with a tasteful celebration during work hours. Have food, drink, kielbasa, whatever works in your team. But tie it to acknowledging a work accomplishment, a completed project, a new grant, record numbers, whatever is happening that's newsworthy. And a great idea is to have employees decide what you are going to do for fun. Just make sure the boss pays for it and brings the food.

Also remember that great managers aren't always the ones to initiate fun, but they certainly allow fun to happen. So that means if you see fun happening—people going out after hours, employees telling jokes, groups getting together for lunch, folks playing ping-pong on break—you encourage it.

Next, effective managers know that the fun should start on an employee's first day. When a new hire joins your team, recognize the stress that person is feeling and lighten the atmosphere with snacks and a welcome card. Take a few minutes as a team to laugh with the new person, perhaps even sharing some of the boneheaded things each team member did when they were new. As you sit and eat and laugh about the mistakes you've all made, there's a good chance the new hire will not only see that she has joined a fun environment, but that it's okay to be human and mess up once in a while. And she also might learn what *not* to do.

As you meet with a new employee, it's important to ask a few simple questions that will help you create an environment that they will consider fun and engaging. Here are a few simple suggestions. Try them out on yourself first:

- If you could write the perfect job description for yourself, what would it be?

  _____

  _____

  _____

- When you have fun at work, what is it you're doing?

  _____

  _____

  _____

- What did you talk about around the water cooler at your last job?

  _____

  _____

  _____

- What would you do on a free day off?

  _____

  _____

  _____

- *How do we bring a sustained sense of fun to our workplace? When we start to have some fun, we quickly lose steam and then it's back to business.*

  _____

  _____

  _____

You may want to reread the introduction to Part II of this book, which talks about creating lasting levity. Simple ways to sustain momentum are to connect with new employees during an effective onboarding process, encourage daily light moments, ask employee teams to create fun events and celebrations, stress effective communication with each individual, and recognize individual and team accomplishments. No one ever said it would be easy to create an engaging workplace, but it's well worth it in returns.

- *I've tried being funny, and it really bombed.*

First understand that the Levity Effect is not so much about being funny as it is about being fun. Give your employees some rope. Enjoy the fun and humor they create. Don't sit in meetings furrowing your brow when employees are making light. Sit back and smile and remind yourself that the resulting effect of their making merry will be making money.

With that said, keep trying to "make a funny" yourself. Having an actual sense of humor and/or the ability to make your people chortle, guffaw, snort, or titter is the cherry on top of the levity cake. Remember, the cake alone is succulent and filling, but the topping is that bit of extra confectionary intake that tantalizes the taste buds and . . . all right, enough. Of course if it's apparent to you that people think you're about as comical as lead poisoning, then realize you may not be the life of the party type—the Bud Abbott, the Chris Farley, the Curly, or the Shemp, for that matter. That's okay. That may be a strength in and of itself. For example, if you're dry then be dry in your wit, like Bob Newhart or Steven Wright. Play to your strengths. Deadpan humor works because it keeps people on their toes. Plus, it's easy for you because you naturally have a fairly emotionless mug. Just make sure your target audience knows when you're joking and when you're serious. It may simply be the difference of slightly raising an eyebrow or adding a barely perceptible grin. Practice a dry comment or two in front of your family around the dinner table or in the car and see if it hits. Use your intelligence, and come up with clever metaphors or inventive and original twists on common conversational conventions. Those can be just as laugh inducing as the one about the guy whose wife was so thin blah, blah, blah. We guarantee you have humor within you. It's just a question of extracting it, which is sort of like whacking the lid of a pickle jar with the handle of a butter knife to get the pickles out. (Please do *not* whack your head with the handle of a butter knife. Thanks, the editor.)

- *You can get too much of a good thing, you know.*

Sure. There's a point where fun crosses the line and threatens your credibility. But let us ask you: Have you ever worked at a place that was too much fun? Where you couldn't get anything done because of the parties and all-around gaiety? Didn't think so.

While this is typically the first fear of a brow-knitting manager, most organizations are hardly in danger of having "too much fun." Said Hitachi High Technology America's Craig Kerkove, senior vice president and general manager of the Semiconductor Equipment Division, "I know if I add 25 percent fun

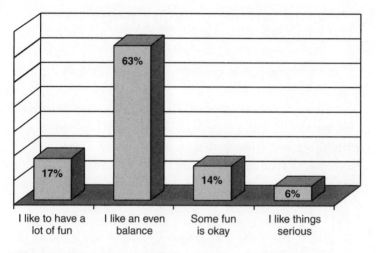

Figure 8.1 Fun at Work. *Source:* ERAC.com Recruiting HR site.

into the day, there's still plenty of pressure and anxiety to go around for everyone."

Most people actually enjoy a mix of fun and serious behavior at work. The trouble is most of us don't get much if any fun on the job. Figure 8.1 shows evidence of what employees are seeking where employees gave their opinions of the balance of fun and serious behavior.

FUN AT WORK

As you can see, more than 94 percent of employees want at least some fun at work. And 80 percent are seeking at least a half-and-half mix. So while your team may not become the next Zappos or Google, you can lighten up a little and give employees what they're looking for—and in turn earn more loyalty, creativity, and productivity.

- *If we have too much fun, people won't take their jobs seriously.*

And if you keep crossing your eyes, they'll stay that way.

The myth of employees distracted by fun is laid to rest by the Great Place to Work® Institute research, which shows the opposite is actually true. Why? Because a fun environment is part of a high-trust environment, and trust is a valuable and precious commodity. Trust is shown to keep employees more loyal, more focused on core values, and more dedicated to your goals as an organization. Not only that, but employees who trust you don't want to lose your trust by missing deadlines or customer demands.

And yet there are still managers who worry that if they have too much fun, it'll be too hard for them to correct employees when necessary. That's only true if the mirth you engage in is overly negative, pessimistic, caustic, sarcastic, and inappropriate— totally opposite to the trust-building levity that is the essence of the Levity Effect. In a later chapter, we'll discuss the Time-and-Place Rule that will help guide you in your levity attempts. But back to the point: Employees take criticism much better from a manager who is lighthearted, respects them, and cares about them as individuals.

Here's a thought on the matter from Jeff Bezos, CEO of Amazon.com, "We have thousands of investors counting on us and we're a team of thousands of employees all counting on each other. That's fun." So here's the CEO of one of the world's fastest-growing companies who is tickled pink by the work they do and the pressure that guides it. Bezos's approach embodies that three-letter word so many are loath to embrace: fun. One more bit of proof that perhaps you too can take your job seriously and still have a blast doing it.

- *We have mandatory fun events around here, and it's no fun at all.*

That may be the sentiment of a few, but typically it's not the case for the majority. For most of us, it's actually nice to do something out of the ordinary for a few minutes during work time. Just because there's a group of malcontents in the back with their arms folded doesn't mean we all have to go out and kick ourselves. The fun is still doing a lot of good for the rest of the team. Some levity has to be manufactured by management. Realize that you are making at least 80 percent of your people happy, and that's a great start. And the other 20 percent will slowly come around. In fact, many of them will enjoy the diversion and get a much-needed laugh (albeit a little sinister) merely by observing what they would define as "childish," or "cheesy," or a "waste of time."

- *My boss tries to make jokes, and we all have to grin and bear it. I wish he'd just grow up.*

There's a two-part answer to this concern. First, to the well-intentioned boss, remember you don't have to be Andy Kaufman. Think more along the lines of Andy Griffith. You don't have to entertain, just create a lighter environment by encouraging fun and laughing at the jokes of others (and occasionally the antics of the town drunk, Otis). Still, if you are set on getting silly, and no one seems to be laughing,

then go back to school. Study humor. Watch comedi-
ans. Practice jokes at home or on a trusted friend
first. And remember that the most effective humor
for a boss is of the self-deprecating variety. Laugh at
yourself, and employees will be very, very happy to
laugh with you.

Second, for the employees who are offended that
their boss is no Steve Martin, lighten up. He or she
is trying to inject some levity into your work life. If
it's offensive and rude, that's another story. But if
it's well-intentioned, keep smiling, and be thankful
that your boss is trying, even if a punch line dies so
miserably that you swear you can hear actual crick-
ets chirping. (Then on his or her birthday, give your
boss a copy of this book.)

- *It's hard to have fun with my team because everyone is remote (or they work shifts).*

When employees are far flung, it does indeed
make things hard for a manager to connect and have
fun. But here's a simple question to ask yourself:
How long does it take you to talk with employees if
they've done something wrong? What, about five
minutes? And yet it can take months for us to say
something nice, make them laugh, or thank them for
a job well done.

In Chapter 6, we showed you how a few companies use technology to keep in touch and have fun
with remote employees and those on various shifts.
Great bosses also do simple things to connect in
human ways: They pick up the phone frequently,
they travel to see their employees, they send regular
handwritten notes or e-mails, they bring employees

into the office for regular meetings and celebrations, they even give people webcams so that they can see each other during meetings. The idea is: Make remote or shift employees realize that you care. And that happens when you, as the important busy boss, take the time to keep in touch.

- *I'm in a serious business. It's just not professional to goof around.*

Sure, that makes sense. Let's end the book right here. Well, except there's the serious airline industry where Southwest seems to have a heck of a lot of fun (and makes a lot of money) sending people into the stratosphere in jet-propelled metal tubes. Oh, and there's the terribly serious health-care industry, where we've worked with numerous organizations, including the number-one-rated health system in the United States to lighten up their leaders, physicians, and supervisors. And there are military contractors, high-tech concerns, manufacturers, government agencies, and others who've asked us to make them laugh and have some fun. In short, it seems lots of smart organizations in some very serious industries are looking to lighten up in ways that work for them.

But what about the superserious world of politics? There's no room for a lighthearted political figure, right? After all, who wants the leader of the free world with one hand on the nuke button and another on a whoopee cushion?

Let's look at just one example. In the 1996 U.S. presidential election race, terribly serious Republican candidate Bob Dole lost to carefree incumbent Bill Clinton. And yet within 48 hours of losing the election, Dole appeared on *The Tonight Show* and *The Late Show* and unleashed a wickedly funny, self-deprecating humor that was thoroughly engaging and surprisingly fresh. As close as the final polls and the actual vote ended, numerous credible political observers believed that if Dole had shown his witty side during the campaign, it may have actually tipped the scales in his favor. Rather than applying levity (post-election fun included a tongue-in-cheek commercial for an erectile dysfunction pill and a guest spot on *Saturday Night Live*), Dole came off as intensely grave and cold in debates and interviews. And when politicians are seen as too serious, they are seen as overly worried, people who could be overwhelmed by high office. Many critics believe that Al Gore and John Kerry also did themselves serious injustices by following the trend of professionalism in their campaigns against George W. Bush (likely never to be confused as stuffy).

Whether you like their politics or not, you can't deny that Bush and Clinton both played up their good ol' boy, down-home, self-effacing images to consecutive terms.

- *We don't have time for fun around here.*

By now, it should be obvious that you don't have time to not have fun. If you want to have a productive, creative, and engaging work experience, you must find the time to cut loose a little. It's that simple. If you don't, you'll end up burning your people out; you won't get their best work, and you'll lose them to competitors.

• *Our budget is way too tight to have fun activities.*

Good news here. Fun is the one management technique that doesn't have to cost a cent, peso, or shekel. In Chapter 7, we listed a shrimp-boat load of fun ideas, many of which cost nothing or very little. Try these, and you may find what many organizations have discovered—that fun can provide a return in new ideas, energy, and satisfaction.

• *My CEO wouldn't go for all this fun stuff.*

Then show her the numbers from Chapter 1; review some of the case studies in the book such as KPMG, Boeing, Nike, Yamaha, Hitachi, and others; and talk about the link to enhanced trust scores, creativity, and productivity. And if your CEO still isn't sold, we know a guy in Jersey.

• *I want to lighten up, but my employees are serious. They don't want to be embarrassed.*

That's just what United Water thought when they asked Scott to speak on employee engagement at a management conference. Some leaders worried about Scott's witty off-the-cuff humor because they were a very conservative water treatment and distribution utility. And, in fact, executives from the French parent company were going to be there, and they certainly would not appreciate levity. But as the presentation started, it was obvious that employees and executives didn't want to be anywhere near as serious as the organizers had worried. The first few shots of levity went over very well, so Scott fired off a few more. Sensing the collective latitude being offered him, Scott started making light of their stuffy environment and even started riffing with a senior officer from France sitting in the front, a man named Michele Trousseau.

Scott deadpanned: "Michele Trousseau, huh? What's that translate to in English? Trousseau—what is that, trousers? Mikey Trousers? Hey everybody, it's Mikey Pants . . . from France." The audience was in hysterics, and Monsieur Trousseau was having the time of his life.

Indeed, after a standing ovation, organizers were quick to ask Scott back for repeated trainings. "We really need to lighten up," the CEO said. "So next time, don't hold back with us. Really let us have it." Not a problem.

What we've seen is that employees in the most serious environments are eager to lighten up if it becomes part of their regular routine and not a one-time event. You may not have Scott's rapier-sharp wit, but your commitment to lightening up will buoy everyone up. It will provide employees with an environment where they are more creative, trusting, and where they communicate more effectively with customers and each other.

With levity, very quickly people will get used to it and begin to appreciate it. Start slowly, do little things to help them acclimate. Copy them on a cartoon that relates to your industry, mention an episode of *The Office* that ties to a work task, have an event to celebrate a work success. Once you are laughing together, you'll see great things happening all around.

- *They'll come to expect fun.*

Yeah . . . and? The great leaders we've profiled in this book have no problem with that at all because they've seen for themselves that fun is linked to performance. They have fun when they're winning. And they win because they have fun. And if you don't mind winning, then there's no problem expecting more fun.

There's no chance of running out of levity, either. Every day you live offers fresh new experiences and material to spur more mirth.

SIDELIGHT
SHOW ME THE FUNNY

8 JOKES TO START A PRESENTATION

Speaking to an important group? Maybe you want to start with something amusing. It actually does work to build rapport and gain their attention. The audience may not fall off their chairs in hysterics (or maybe they will), but we guarantee they'll appreciate the break from the humdrum with these simple funny starters. Use these if you are:

1. *The unwilling speaker:* An oil tycoon invites a group of people to his mansion. He greets the guests standing in front of a 30-meter swimming pool filled with hungry Great White sharks. He explains that anyone brave enough to swim the length of the pool can either marry his beautiful daughter or receive half his oil wealth. Suddenly, he hears splashing in the pool and sees a young man frantically swimming.

The man splashes and thrashes and finally reaches the other end, where he throws himself out onto the deck. The billionaire runs over, astounded. "Young man," he says, "I am thrilled by your bravado. Would you want to marry my daughter?" "No," says the young man. "Well then you must want half my oil wealth?" Again, the young man declines. "Then what do you *want?*" asks the tycoon. The young man looks up with a stern expression. "I want the name of the jerk who threw me into the pool." (The business connection is made when you talk about the person who asked you to speak, and you say, "I know who threw me into this pool, and I'm going to get him.")

2. *Speaking on communication:* A rich old man is nearing the end of his life, and he is attended on his death bed by his wife. As the last hour approaches, the old man has an epiphany and begs his wife to bury him with all of his money. "I don't want the kids to squander my millions. Bury me with my money, and I will die a happy man." Of course his wife pleads that she and the children need the riches to maintain their lifestyle, but he is relentless. Eventually she gives in and says, "All right. I'll bury you with all of your money." And indeed, at the funeral she is seen placing a box inside the coffin of her late husband. One of her friends approaches her after the ceremony and asks, "Sylvia, you can't be serious. You really buried him with all of his money?" "Of course," the wife replies, "I keep my word. I said I'd bury him with all of his money. So

yesterday I took all of his money and put it in my account and then I wrote him a check. And if he can cash it where he's going, well then more power to him." (This is a great joke about the gray areas in business to begin any address about clarity of communication, keeping our promises/word, building trust, or integrity, and so on.)

3. *Talking about the need to be flexible/change:* This is the transcript of a radio conversation between the British and the Irish off the coast of Kerry, October 1998:

Irish: Please divert your course 15 degrees to the South to avoid a collision.

British: Recommend you divert your course 15 degrees to the North to avoid a collision.

Irish: Negative. You will have to divert your course 15 degrees to the South to avoid a collision.

British: This is the Captain of a British Navy Ship. I say again, divert *your* course.

Irish: Negative. I say again, you will have to divert *your* course.

British: This is the aircraft carrier HMS BRITIANNIA! The second largest ship in the British Atlantic fleet! We are accompanied by three destroyers, three cruisers, and numerous support vessels! I demand you change your course 15 degrees North! I say again, that is 15 degrees North or countermeasures will be undertaken to ensure the safety of this ship!

Irish: We are a lighthouse. . . . Your call.

(This was actually not a real conversation, but it's important to set it up as if it were and then disclose the urban legend. However, it's a wonderfully light way to begin a discussion of change management topics.)

4. *Speaking about health care:* It is a sad day at the hospital as a long-time cardiologist is bid farewell. At his funeral, no expense is spared, and indeed at the funeral home is a massive wreath of red roses in the shape of a heart. After the final prayer is offered, the coffin is wheeled out and amazingly the heart-shaped wreath opens, and the coffin passes through the middle in a final, symbolic gesture of the cardiologist's life work. The room is silent except for a few muffled sobs. But then, from the back of the room, a man cannot contain himself any longer and burst into laughter. "Oh, I'm so sorry," says the man. "I didn't mean any disrespect. I was just thinking about my own funeral. You see, I'm a proctologist."

5. *Talking about relationships:* A husband and wife are driving through the countryside when their conversation turns animated and quickly deteriorates into an argument. Eventually the woman stops speaking to her husband entirely. The man, not to be outdone, notices they are passing a barnyard inhabited by pigs. "Relatives of yours?" he smugly asks. "Yes," she says. "In-laws."

6. *A flight attendant:* "We're sorry for the delay, but our automated bag smasher is broken and we are having to break your bags by hand. We apologize for the inconvenience. But in the meantime, you may be thrilled to hear that someone on the plane is turning 100 today. So as you are deplaning, you may wish the pilot a happy birthday." (Told to us by a very funny Skywest Airlines flight attendant.)

7. *Teaching people not to cut corners:* There was a house painter named Glen who thinned down his paint to make it go further. Eventually his local church decided to do a big restoration job. Glen put in a bid, and, because his price was so low, he got the work. He set about erecting the scaffolding, buying the paint and, yes, I am sorry to say, thinning it down with paint thinner. Well, Glen was up on the scaffolding, painting away, the job nearly completed, when suddenly there was a horrendous clap of thunder, the sky opened, and rain poured down washing the thinned paint from the entire church and knocking Glen clear off the scaffold to land on the lawn among the gravestones, surrounded by telltale puddles of the thinned and useless paint. Glen was no fool. He knew this was a judgment from the Almighty, so he got down on his knees and cried: "Oh, God, forgive me; what should I do?" And from the thunder, a mighty voice spoke: "Repaint! Repaint! And thin no more!" (A bit corny, but they'll laugh and the moral is obvious. We don't cut corners around here. We take care of our customers.)

8. *Talking about outsmarting the competition:* A beautiful woman and a man are involved in a car accident on a snowy, cold morning. Neither of them is hurt although both cars are demolished. After they crawl out of the wreckage, the woman says, "Wow, just look at our cars! There's nothing left, but we're unhurt. This must be a sign that we should meet." Flattered, the man replies, "Oh yes, I agree with you completely, this must be a sign!" The woman continues, "And look at this, here's another miracle. My car is demolished but this bottle of wine didn't break. Surely God wants us to drink this wine, celebrate our good fortune, and see where the evening leads." She hands the bottle to the man. He nods in eager agreement, opens the bottle, drinks half of it, and then hands it back to the woman. The woman immediately puts the cap back on and hands the bottle back to the man. The man asks, "Aren't you having any?" The woman replies, "No. I think I'll just wait for the police." (A good way to begin a discussion about how we need be smarter and more creative than the other guys.)

CHAPTER NINE

Levity for Life

Bringing Home the Fun

Peter Parker leads a double life. On the one hand, he's a bright college kid with good grades, a cute girlfriend, and a job shooting photos for the city newspaper. On the other hand, he's the Amazing Spider-Man swinging from webs, nabbing crooks, and saving the free world, well, New York City anyway. An enviable existence, wouldn't you think? So, why is he always so miserable, gloomy, and in need of a good prescription medication? Because he leads a double life. He's two faced. It's the age-old problem of the duality of (spider)man. In one of the Spidey flicks, Peter's good side literally battled against his inherent evil side. Of course his good side also battled a 20-story sand mutant and a turncoat, disfigured best friend. But, don't we all?

After speaking to a large group of managers at Michelin, one of the employees told us an interesting story. He said his boss lived in the same neighborhood as one of his friends. This employee had been shocked to find out that his boss was known as the "party guy" of the neighborhood. Everybody thought he was the funniest guy on the block, and they all wanted to hang out with him. If the boss was going to the neighborhood barbecue, then you'd want to be there, too. This was jaw-dropping news to this employee because his experiences with his boss were anything *but* a party. His boss consistently drained positive energy from the room with his excruciating seriousness.

Sound at all familiar? We're often surprised to discover the *real* people we work with when we mingle at company parties and off-site events. Latent gold mines of humor are unearthed in nonwork surroundings such as golf courses, amusement parks, and massage parlors.

How about the flip side of the coin purse? Debbie is an outgoing, witty, and personable boss. Her employees and others simply *must* seek her out each morning to hear the latest buzz, have a good laugh, and sample some of her contagious energy. She is tolerant of mistakes and encourages improvement. Her leadership style is laced with levity. She sets a great tone for the whole workplace.

But at home Debbie is a total opposite. She is apathetic or even negative. She belittles her husband and children and has no time for fun and games. People adore her at work, and avoid her at home.

And, just like Peter Parker, she swings from webs and doles out vigilante justice . . . no wait—

And, just like Peter Parker, she endures internal turmoil, whether she's aware of it or not. The battle between "work Debbie" and "home Debbie" rages on. And if Debbie's not careful, she may soon burn out in both worlds. She expends so much energy being magnanimous and gracious to her employees that she has precious few drops of cheer left for her family, the people in her life who deserve her very best treatment. Debbie will never be truly happy until she finds some consistency between the two personalities inside of her; she must become the same person at home that she is at work and vice versa. At that point, she'll reconnect with her family and friends, and the kids will stop referring to her as "that bitty who makes breakfast sometimes."

A wise man once said, "No other success can compensate for failure in the home." That's the beauty of the Levity Effect. It isn't just for work. It affects all aspects of life. Just like *Oprah.*

Craig Kerkove, senior vice president and general manager of a division of Hitachi High Technologies, told us, "I try to lighten up the home environment. With my wife and son, the three of us go to movies together, dinner together. We hang out as a pack. I like my job. I like being here. You have to try to have fun and enjoy the people you work with. But when the job is done, I look forward to going home and hanging out with those guys (the family) too."

Here's the part we really like: "No one ever retires and gets close to the end of their life and says, 'Gee, I wish I'd spent more time at work,'" Kerkove said.

A huge part of lightening up around the workplace is understanding that people have lives outside of work and they aren't constantly thinking about their jobs. According to a recent poll publicized by Ken Blanchard, employees say that having a boss who is sympathetic to their personal (outside of work) issues is the third most important factor in their work experience, right after feeling "in on things" and a "full appreciation for work done" (number one). It's time to get past the days of cantankerous timekeepers who raise an eyebrow at every unaccounted-for microsecond of an 80-hour pay period or simply *must* know where an employee could possibly be going at a quarter to five? Here's how this plays out in most organizations.

> [Shannon is packing up her bag and cleaning up her area. She logs off her computer, stretches, looks around nervously, extracts her car keys from her bag, and rises. It's 3:30 PM. She sheepishly bids farewell to those nearest her cubicle.]
>
> **Shannon:** Well, I've got to get going. My son is coming home from Iraq this afternoon, and I want to be sure to be there to greet him at the baggage carousel.
>
> [Her coworkers react suspiciously, eyeing her cautiously.]
>
> **Dick:** Soooo . . . you're leaving early then? Wow (looking at clock) . . . in the threes still.
>
> **Shannon:** (apologetically) Yeah, I know, but . . . it's pretty important.
>
> [An administrative type, Flemberta, approaches and sees Shannon with her car keys and packed bag.]
>
> **Flemberta:** Ho-ho! Look who's quitting on us early today! Can't stick it out the full nine hours, eh? Heh heh. You ran this past Hannerhan, right?
>
> **Shannon:** Uhh . . . not officially, no. Was I supposed to? I mean, I mentioned it at lunch. My boy's been deployed for 18 months now; I thought everybody knew he was coming home today.

Dick: What about the four o'clock meeting on the new stapler policy? You skipping that? Prit-tee lame if you're askin' . . .

Shannon: I'm in a bit of a hurry; I'll see you all to-morrow.

Flemberta: So, you'll be in at what, six-thirty? To make up for the time?

This entire scenario could play itself out so much easier in an atmosphere of trust and respect, a work-place governed by a leader, such as yourself, who al-lows people the common courtesy of having an actual life outside of work. Admittedly, the preceding vi-gnette is a bit far-fetched. A bit. Sure we exaggerated the problem with the whole military homecoming angle, but it helps drive home the point. At the heart of the Levity Effect is a simple axiom: Lighten up.

And for that to legitimately occur, it can't simply be manufactured. True levity is an attitude, a sense, a part of who you are. You carry it with you every-where you go. Like a tattoo. Here then are a few ideas for completing the circle of your levity efforts and becoming more consistent in your approach, at work or elsewhere.

LIGHTEN UP AT HOME

Start Each Day Smiling in the Mirror

It's old school, sure, but keep up the daily routine, and pretty soon it'll become an actual grin, not sim-ply a forced exercise. Smiling is contagious even when it's just your own reflection beaming back at you. It may sound oversimplified and cheesy, and your significant other may suspect you need couch time with Niles Crane, but just try it. The mere movement of the smile and laughter muscles, especially when atrophied from woeful underuse, can actually trigger an emotional response. You literally can raise your spirits and change your mood simply by *beginning* to grin. Stay smiling and staring at your reflection as long as needed to cheer yourself up and feel good. We could mention the usefulness of chanting positive affirmations and cheering yourself on, but let's not go New Age.

Smile at Your Family

You've stepped out of the bathroom and your reflective little happy fest; now, extend it to those people who actually matter more than you do. Remember, you're trying to create a positive and consistent balance between work and life, so extend to your loved ones the same courtesies you'll extend to your officemates later in the day. Shock your housemates by greeting them with smile-laced "good mornings." They may not care, especially the teens who'll think you're a nut job, but you'll feel great. And if you live alone, well, you can always smile at the neighbor's family through the window, but could you throw on a bathrobe first? This is a decent neighborhood.

Spend Time with Your Peeps

Eat dinner with your family around the table. Tell stories about your day's amusing adventures. Take the time to talk and laugh about everyday life. Sacrifice some of *your* time for them. Go to kids' ball games, movies, and school events. Heaven forbid you should show up a little late for work because you spent a few minutes at the elementary school watching your kids stumble in their pilgrim shoes in a Thanksgiving skit. Take a walk around the neighborhood with your significant other. Have a water fight when washing the car. Learn to rollerblade. The better you get at having, allowing, and supporting fun at home, the easier and more natural it will be at work.

Go Easy on the Kids

They're going to screw up. They're going to make you sick with worry. They won't make their beds. They don't want to eat that green stuff. They'll torment their siblings. They'll test your resolve to never spank them. They won't clean up after the puppy after swearing that they would. They'll refuse to shower. They'll shower too much. They'll take your money. *And lie about it!* Still, don't blow a fuse. Have a sense of perspective. Will the world end? Isn't this their job as kids? To make your forehead veins throb and pulsate? Yes. Relax the jaw. Unknit the brow. Kids do this stuff. You did. Dig way down deep in there and conjure up a laugh about it. It may feel like the least natural and counterintuitive reaction you can imagine, but what's done is done, so what good is raging like a college basketball coach?

Go Easy on Your Sweetheart

Would your significant other be surprised to hear you in a conversation with your employees? Would he or she be baffled or even hurt observing the attention you pay, the interest you convey, or the pleasantries you say to Phil or Tina in accounting, but never to anyone at home? By the same token, would your employees think aliens had replaced you with a clone if they visited you at home and witnessed you wrestling and laughing with your kids?

Take Stock

Today at work, note how you instinctively treat those around you. See how likely you are to communicate with respect and deference. Ask yourself throughout the day, "Do I do the same for my husband /wife/boyfriend/girlfriend/kids/roommate/livestock back at the house?" Challenge yourself today to go home and treat your spouse like a potential new hire. The most useful and truly happy leaders at work are those whose gap between their work persona and home persona is the narrowest. Consistency is king. Or at the very least a member of the royal kitchen staff.

LIGHTEN UP IN PUBLIC

Smile at Strangers

We travel a lot. At least once a week, we're out speaking to management groups all over the world. Have you ever walked through ATL (Atlanta's Hartfield-Jackson Airport) at, well, any time of day? It is the definition of "teeming." When was the last time you can remember seeing anyone, ever, on the train between Concourse B and C with even half a grin? Travelers do not smile. It's some kind of universally understood arrangement. No smiling. And no liquids except in a quart-size plastic sandwich bag that may not contain an actual sandwich. The same rule of despair holds true for passengers at LAX, JFK, ORD,

EWR, DFW, PDX, PHX, LAS, SLC, and, of course, FAT (but they're just bitter). You will of course see some smiles at MCO, especially on arrival . . . the kids are so excited.

But we digress. Walk with a smile on your face. We *dare* you. (Now you can't refuse.) It doesn't have to be, and shouldn't be, a full, toothy, open-mouthed smile. Just a grin. A smile in your eyes. After all, those are the best smiles anyway. If your eyes aren't smiling, chances are the smile will look painted on, insincere, and possibly evil. (Think Jack Nicholson's "Here's Johnny!" smile from *The Shining*). But regardless of others' reactions, you'll feel good simply by virtue of being a trailblazer and standing out a little, bucking the norm.

Shopping malls, grocery stores, sporting events, church services—wherever you find yourself, remember to shoot for consistency. Smile at people and give them a little head nod as you pass. Work extra hard to remember and then use people's names when greeting them. What a difference a little thing like a pleasant "hello" backed by an authentic and warm smile can do to perk up someone's spirits—in most cases your own. The cumulative effect of these morsels of mirth is incalculable. Happiness is viral, contagious.

Lighten Up on Vacation

It is time off after all. There are no deadlines, no meetings, and no numbers to run. Everyone knows there are going to be long lines on cruise ships or at museums and amusement parks. Why fight it? Keep a smile on your face and perspective. Surprise yourself and your spouse or kids by *not* blowing a gasket when seeing the lines wind three miles past the "Wait from this point: 45 minutes," sign. Settle down on airplanes. There are going to be delays. And guess what? Nearly all of them will be about keeping you from dying. Keep your audible sighs and groans to yourself when the pilot informs you that we'll be at the gate for a few minutes while mechanics try to replace the light bulb in the lavatory. Somehow, we're pretty sure, that light helps keep that 100-ton plane 40,000 feet above the earth.

Lighten Up at Public Events

Remember football, basketball, even hockey games are for *entertainment* purposes, and while we all want our team to win, there is literally only a 50/50 chance that it'll happen, less if you root for the Cubs. Laugh and have fun, even if your team is getting waxed. You can still be entertained even during a loss. We occasionally will draw mean stares and boos from fans when we react positively to a spectacular play by the *other* team . . . the enemy. It doesn't change the fact that we love our team, but holy cow that was an impressive fingertip grab for a touchdown!

Lighten Up in Traffic

Literally no one on the road has anything personal against you. They could not possibly care less about you. They care about themselves. Be the courteous one. Let people into your lane. Use your turn signal. Slow down in inclement weather. Smile and wave (all five fingers). Consider subscribing to satellite radio and listening to comedy channels. We usually have XM or Sirius satellite radio in our rental cars and channel 151 is Laugh USA—family-clean stand-up comics. We've had to drive to some remote speaking engagements, and having comedy on the radio makes the time fly by. Howls of laughter put us in a great mood.

LIGHTEN UP IN RESTAURANTS

Treat the wait staff with some respect. They're not your temporary slaves. Sure, the best servers know how to fade into the background and anticipate your needs, but for those who won't win server-of-the-year awards, cut them some slack. You probably dine out to have a good time. Don't allow minor flairs of incompetence or undercooked entrees put a damper on a fun evening. Handle issues directly and respectfully. You'll stand a better chance of avoiding mystery ingredients in your soufflé if you ease up on the disgruntled guest routine. (For the truly obnoxious servers wearing chips on their shoulders or shamelessly fishing for tips, all bets are off. Let 'em have it.)

LIGHTEN UP IN PRIVATE
(SO TO SPEAK)

Take Better Care of Yourself

Have a regular exercise routine. If your knees can handle it, get out and walk or jog regularly. If they can't, swim or ride a bike. People who regularly sweat, grunt, and breathe heavy are less likely to get depressed, sustain an injury, or go "Russell Crowe" on hotel desk clerks or coworkers for that matter.

Develop Tolerance for Others' Misguided Attempts at Humor

Don't be too quick to mete out judgment or chastisement when people around you shoot off inappropriate humor or fail to make others laugh. Most cases of someone being offended are not intentional. Being offended is not a condition that is imposed on you. It is a choice you make. Quickly forgive and forget the occasional poor-taste remark, knowing full well that you are likely to launch an equally lame line yourself eventually.

Work on Your Sense of Humor

Remember that it is yours and yours alone. It is incredibly rare that any two people will laugh at all the same things. Or express humor the same way. When we've spoken to large groups, we've presented a few quick comedy clips from movies or television shows and then had the audience rate them from funniest to least funny. Recently in a room of 600 people, only 4 had the same list.

It is our belief that what the world needs now is levity, sweet levity (Everybody sing!). We could all afford to lighten up a little. Don't get us wrong. There is always a need for dignified, well-mannered social interactions. We're not suggesting that every day be Casual Day or that people run amok planting plastic vomit or scheming daily practical jokes. We're simply saying: Let there be moderation, a little balance. The effects of levity—creativity, productivity, prosperity, and so on—are more easily produced by the person who brings that balance into all facets of his or her life.

SideLight
Getting Lighter

3 Steps to Developing Your Own
Unique Sense of Humor

Everyone can be funnier. Here are some simple ways to engage and expand your humorous side:

1. *Exposure:* Watch movies and read books that offer a variety of comedy styles. Broaden your horizons and sample from different genres: slapstick, parody, irony, British, intellectual, farce, situational, sophomoric, and so on. Watch what others find funny. Rent the top film comedies of the year or check out the top 10 rated sitcoms on TV this week. Give them a chance. There's probably a good reason why so many people watch them. You may not be attracted to some shows simply from their teasers, promos, and previews. Watch them anyway. You don't have to love them; you may even hate them. You may be surprised at something you just knew you'd hate, but instead, you ended up laughing so hard your nose bled. It's a refreshing realization when you discover unexpected sources of laughter.

   Observe and remember the humor in your day-to-day experiences. Look for things that are relatable to other people. All the best comics simply tell you something you already knew from your own experience. And you laugh. "It's funny because it's true!" Homer

Simpson once declared. (Yeah, yeah, we know he's fictional.) But he's right. Keep it relatable and local.

Read, read, read. The more you read comedy or satire, the more saturated your brain becomes with wittier dialogue and comical expressions. A leader who can pepper his or her language with interesting, obscure, and funny-sounding words and metaphors not only seems funnier but smarter, too.

2. *Inventory:* As you discover what you find amusing, take note of it. Remember it. File it away. Film director Neil LaBute (*Nurse Betty, Possession*), whose innate and legendary sense of humor belies some of the more serious works he's produced, once told us that he imagines his brain as a filing cabinet. When he comes across something humorous—a joke, a quip, a funny word—that could be useful later, he mentally files it away and then draws on it as needed. This is part of what makes a comic genius, a good memory. The other part is timing and discretion. That's two parts actually, but nobody said you had to be a math whiz to be a comic genius.

On the off chance that you aren't blessed with total recall, make a habit of carrying a notebook or, if dexterity is your gift, a PDA to jot down ideas and bits of humor as you are exposed to them. Ninety percent of truly funny stuff out there has been lifted anyway. Somebody else said it, and it got passed along. Now it's up to you to apply those gems in the proper setting and context for maximum payout.

3. *Application:* Here's where it gets tricky. You've exposed yourself to humor, determined what fits best for you, and armed yourself with some mirth nuggets; now go fire them off. Practice in safe environs—at home, with close friends, or underwater. Just remember the basic rule of jocularity: when in doubt . . . test it first in an offense-free environment. But generally speaking, your attempts to deliver appropriate (see the conclusion) levity will be met warmly. Most members of the human family, bless their hearts, are gracious humor receivers and have no desire to see anyone's feelings hurt by not offering at least a gratuitous giggle. Over time, the sympathy laughs will evolve into genuine blasts of gusto; so don't give in too easily.

Here's an example of dead-on Exposure, Inventory, and Application from Adrian's 11-year-old son, Tony, at an amusement park restaurant. He had ordered the nachos, attracted by the mouthwatering picture displayed by the register. The photograph showed a mound of crunchy nachos pilled high with three cheeses, peppers, olives, salsa, and other fixings. When the nachos arrived, however, they were not as advertised. Instead he received ten chips stacked sideways in a plastic container with a tub of melted yellow goop. He stoically ate the dry, tasteless lunch, regretting his decision quietly. As the family picked up to leave, Tony smiled up at the grumpy teenage cashier and said, "My compliments to the photographer."

We all burst out laughing. Even the cashier managed a knowing chuckle.

Now, that was obviously a funny line he'd been exposed to from a comedian at some time in his past, but he'd inventoried it and had applied it at the right time and place. And if an 11-year-old can do it, we all can.

CONCLUSION

Your Levity IQ

You're ready now—take a deep breath—to assess yourself. Have you put on a few pounds? Do your eyebrows need trimming? Ever heard of white strips? Would it kill you to vacuum your car out? Sorry, too personal. Let's back out a bit and see how well you're coming along in the area of levity by administering a little quiz. In earlier chapters, we discussed examples of office humor, the positive and negative effects of having a good time in the workplace, and with any luck, demonstrated how a dynamic, enjoyable, and productive atmosphere can be created with just a bit of focused fun.

There are one or two downsides. You face the very real possibility that your attempt or two at fun will fall flat, backfire, or even be met by chilly, blank stares.

Still, you have to acknowledge that the statistics don't lie. Keeping employees happy and productive, retaining them, and maintaining their best effort is worth the gamble of an occasional bomb.

Even the *Harvard Business Review* reports that executives with a sense of humor climb the corporate ladder more quickly and earn more money than their counterparts.

What's at stake if we ignore this call to lighten up? Not much, if business as usual is good enough. The trouble is, your competitors are getting better every day, and you need to improve as well. And part of the missing piece of the puzzle of higher-employee engagement, retention, innovation, and energy can be as simple as the Levity Effect.

On to the quiz. Don't worry; it's not timed. And neatness doesn't count. We won't report your score to your mother. In fact, we won't know your score at all because this is a book you're reading, and we can't transcend the rules of time and space . . . yet. So, we'll give you a few examples of humorous exchanges between people, and you (1) predict the consequence of the event, and (2) rate the following for their appropriateness. Here's something else to consider: Do these attempts at humor respect what we call the Time-and-Place Rule? That is, are they made at the right time and in the right place? We'd all be wise to memorize this simple statement: the *Time-and-Place Rule* is defined as

> the universally ignored law that dictates that before any workplace humor is executed, its bearer must determine, using reasonably sound judgment, if said humor is appropriate for both the physical setting and the space in time which it occupies.

So, are you ready?

1. A middle-school principal has a squirming seventh-grader in his office. The principal looks

sternly at the boy who knows he's in big trouble. The principal stares at the boy and asks, "Do you have any idea what you've done?" The boy— blessed with the ability to give snappy come- backs—says, "Why? Don't you know either? And you call yourself a principal."

2. A married couple goes to the mall so the wife can buy some new clothes. The husband, less than enthusiastic about sitting outside of a dressing room, settles in for an afternoon of torture. "Do these jeans make my butt look big?" she asks at one point. The husband re- flexively mutters, "No. Your butt makes your jeans look big."

3. A male boss goes up to his female employee. He says, "Hey Claire, come here for a second, I've got something I need to show you." "What is it?" she asks. The boss hands her a box, "I bought something for my wife for our anniver- sary, and I'm worried it may not fit. You're about her size. Would you mind trying it on? Or at least holding it up to you?" Inside the box is sexy lingerie.

4. At a team meeting, the leader of the discus- sion stands up and tries to break the ice by saying, "I hope this joke won't offend any- body." (That's all you need to know.)

5. It's Halloween, and the boss walks into a cor- porate meeting wearing a werewolf mask. He howls at the fluorescent light and has a big laugh. He's forgotten that, a few weeks earlier, Janet's daughter was eaten by wolves.

6. The same werewolf boss goes to the water- cooler, puts on the mask, and says, "I'm just

not feeling like myself today." He explodes in
laughter again. He has recently announced
that there will be no holiday bonuses.

7. At a meeting near year-end, one leader tries to
   make the point that the annual holiday gift
   should be something more memorable than
   in years' past. "After all," he asks one young
   woman. "Do you remember what you got for
   Christmas two years ago?" She says, "I'm Jewish." And after the room goes silent, he says,
   "Well then, do you remember what you got
   for Easter?"

Not a difficult quiz, was it?

We like to think that humor is subjective, that if
we say something and nobody laughs, well, they just
didn't get it; they don't have a sense of humor.

Or maybe it's a time-and-place issue.

We witnessed the last example firsthand as we
were conducting research. It was painfully obvious
that the boss quickly realized his mistake with the
Jewish employee. The few seconds after his gaffe
were pretty intense. But he knew his audience. Fur-
thermore, he knew they respected him. How did they
respond when he came back with his comment about
Easter? Initially, they were shocked, but it only
lasted a second. All of a sudden, the woman laughed,
and the entire room joined in.

He messed up. Out of ignorance, he made an un-
thinking remark that might have been divisive or
even hurtful. He might have tried an apology, but
who knows if it would have solved the problem. He
used levity and showed that they needn't take everything too seriously. His joke signaled that he had
been insensitive, but also that nothing was to be

taken personally. They forgave him (and their gen-uine laughter was the proof of that) because they re-spected his attempt to keep things light.

A FEW RED FLAGS

For leaders who wish to dip their toes into the pool of levity, here are four quick areas to avoid:

1. *Kidding:* Statements that come out of your mouth followed by the words "just kidding" are usually a mistake. Often, people who say hurtful things do it on purpose, so try not to join that crowd.

2. *Mockery:* A mean-spirited joke at someone's expense hurts everyone involved. In addition to the person being mocked, all listeners im-mediately know that they are fair game too for the next round of attacks, and this atmo-sphere of combat radiates tension and dis-trust. Mockery has no place on the job or at home. Siblings and spouses are especially prone to these tugs-of-war of derision.

3. *Sarcasm:* Some things are better left unsaid. Certainly the day-to-day work environment is rife with opportunities to let loose with cyni-cal tirades. Just because those opportunities rise up and present themselves like a man-drill in heat doesn't mean you have to seize them.

4. *Anger:* Humor is a release of tension, but when it's also a release of anger it's not funny. When you have an impulse to *get back at* somebody with a joke, then all of a sudden, its goal has shifted away from the purposes of

this book: unity and cooperation. And sadly, you're headed for the kind of humor that is anything but light.

EXAMPLES OF DOING IT RIGHT

Humor can be aimed at people and still be appropriate. One of the goals of levity is to bring people together, so a vague lightness won't work as well as something that is tailored to individuals and specific situations. Here's an example we saw. We were observing a meeting that a Levity Effect leader chaired to understand how he engendered such commitment from his employees. As we sat quietly to the side, we noticed the meeting taking an interesting turn as a long list of duties was being assigned to the newest employee, Trish. The leader obviously noticed her face getting more and more worried, but he said little as the team members unloaded their unwanted tasks on her shoulders. Finally, he kindly stopped everyone for a moment by holding up a hand. "Trish," he smiled at her, "Are you starting to feel like Luke Skywalker in the trash compactor?"

The group burst into authentic laughter not only at his Jedi wisdom, but at the leader's adept reading of the situation. Trish smiled and nodded. The leader didn't need to say anything more. From that moment on, the group backed off, even took back some of the assigned work, and Trish visibly relaxed.

Humor like this is insightful and concise. In this case, the leader sized up a problem and quickly improved the situation with a single humorous remark. He didn't have to insult the team members who were piling it on. He didn't have to lecture them and, by so doing, create an us-versus-them environment. He just made a joke that gave everyone a fresh perspective. Done.

Levity means lightness after all, as in "lighten up." We witnessed a good example in a financial services company, where we watched a levity leader deal deftly with a grumpy CFO in a tense planning meeting. The CFO was grudgingly admitting that he might have been initially wrong about funding a particular project and that he would now consider supporting it if his long list of demands were met. He was hardly rolling over, and there was a lot of negotiation ahead, but there was a glimmer of hope for those who believed the project could provide substantial revenue gains for the organization.

It was the levity leader who broke the awkward silence. She asked: "So, Bob, you're telling us there actually *is* a snowball in hell?" Even the CFO hooted, and the group began on a positive note to discuss how to implement necessary changes.

That story reveals that humor has a way of settling scores. But it can do it without lingering resentment. It reminds us of a famous Winston Churchill story. In 1945, though Churchill was instrumental in helping the Allies win World War II, he lost his reelection bid for Prime Minister. When the news came out, Churchill was said to be taking a bath. He remarked through the door, "They have a perfect right to kick me out. That is democracy."

And yet when he was offered the Order of the Garter, he asked, "Why should I accept the Order of the Garter when the British people have just given me the Order of the Boot?" For all that he had accomplished, he had every reason to be bitter. Fortunately,

he kept his sense of humor even in trying circumstances and was back at the reins in 1951.

Recently, in a company's managers meeting that
we attended to observe a levity-minded leader, the new
snooty name of the remodeled company cafeteria was
announced. The administrative vice president was
thrilled to congratulate the winner whose suggestion
had been selected from hundreds of entries and explained that the lucky contributor would be treated to
a month of free lunches, to which the levity leader in
the back of the room asked, "Where?" The laughter
among the 100 or so managers was actually deafen-
ing. Later, many of the meeting attendees were still
laughing at the well-timed, one-word query. "That was
so funny, I mean it *is* cafeteria food," one said. "It's
great to have someone here who's willing to say stuff
like that. A lot of us think it, but we won't say it." Oh,
and here's the best part. The administrative VP over
the cafeteria laughed at it as well. With a thick skin
and a healthy sense of levity, she played along and enjoyed the moment, understanding the value of a little
self-effacement for the overall well-being of the team.

FALSE ASSUMPTIONS

One last piece of Levity Effect guidance: Sometimes,
people fail to make levity work for themselves because they give up too easily. After a failed attempt,
they stop. Their initial impulse is to reshelve the levity tool next to their band saw and electric sander.
We think they would be better served by trying to
figure out what went wrong.

The number-one reason humor backfires at
work is that a businessperson makes the dangerous

assumption that everyone is like he or she is. It's easy to assume that everyone has our sense of humor, to believe that a person will react the way we would, to think that anyone who looks like us has the same values and beliefs. Here are a few of the most common forms of this assumption—and why they don't work:

"She has no sense of humor." Not true. We've been around the globe a time or two, have spoken in India, China, England, Germany, Singapore, Greece, South Africa, Spain, Korea, Omaha, and a host of other countries, and we have yet to meet a person without a sense of humor. Alas, we've met many people who don't share our particular brand of humor. Go figure. But laughter really is universal.

"I hope this doesn't offend anyone." Few of us would think that because we preface a kick with, "I hope this doesn't hurt," it would give us permission to boot someone. But often, we think a warning to our colleagues that we are about to say something risqué alleviates us from its impact. This preface doesn't let us off the hook in a work environment. If you think it might offend someone, save it for the Friday night bowling league.

"But I thought we were the same." We were in a meeting once where the leader looked around the room, noticed there were no individuals of Asian descent present, and proceeded to tell a very racist joke. What he didn't realize is that his customer—also in the room—was the proud mother of a darling Chinese girl. Needless to say, this

humorous attempt backfired, and the manager had to eat serious crow to repair the relationship.

"But we were at lunch." Just because we've left the building doesn't mean we've left our work roles behind. Managers, in particular, may fall prey to the temptation to show their employees that, outside of work, they can party hardy with the best of them. The problem is that their employees often don't understand the same distinction between work and play and may see a manager's inappropriately rowdy humor at happy hour as permission to repeat it in the office first thing Monday morning.

NOW, GO AND LIGHTEN UP

Leading with levity is about developing a lightness of manner. Levity is equated with having a *sense* of humor. Too many people wrongly assume that a sense of humor means you're hilarious. Not necessarily. Very few hilarious people walk the same work halls at the same time. The Levity Effect is aimed at the majority of us who simply possess or wish to develop a stronger sense of humor, in the hopes that it will help us develop into more effective leaders.

Now, we've all worked for a brow knitter or jaw clencher at one point in our careers, and you know that the resulting atmosphere is claustrophobic, morale is low, production suffers, and attrition is rampant. After all, how fun or easy is it to work with people who are wound tighter than Jerry Falwell at a gay pride parade?

So what do you do when you work for a grump? After all, that's who signs the paychecks. We end up remaining silent. Oh, we want to say something all right. If only we could speak up. It reminds us of this little nugget from the Bill Murray movie, *Stripes*, as the character Sgt. Hulka (played by Warren Oates) and other recruits are introduced to an intense wiry fellow who likes to be called Psycho:

Psycho: The name's Francis Sawyer, but everybody calls me Psycho. Any of you guys call me Francis, and I'll kill you.

And I don't like nobody touching my stuff! So just keep your meat hooks off.

If I catch any of you guys in my stuff, I'll kill you. Also, I don't like nobody touching me. Now, any of you (guys) touch me, I'll kill you.

Sgt. Hulka: Lighten up, Francis.

That says it all, doesn't it? Lighten up. So, as a final exercise, to better cope with the inevitable grouches around you, wherever you are right now, laugh out loud. Come on, just do it. See what happens. Tighten your gut and push out a guffaw. Where are you right at this very moment? On a bus? In your cubicle? At home? On an airplane? Would it be terribly wrong for you to laugh right now?

Tilt your head back and let a laugh rip. It may sound fake or put on. So what? Within seconds you'll feel a surge of authentic joy, possibly coupled with a degree of humiliation and shame. But you won't care, because that natural little rush is worth it.

And with any luck you'll *infect* someone else with your little laugh. It may spread a little among those around you, as infections do. When you hear a great laugh, it gets you going, doesn't it?

Oh sure, your little fit might be met with animosity by one or two. Perhaps seated across from you in the doctor's waiting room is a fully enraged jaw clencher named Frank. You know his name because he still hasn't taken off his work ID badge; that's only removed for the occasional shower. He's burning a hole through you with his deadly serious glare. And you can just read in his eyes, "Cut the laughs, pal, this is a podiatrist's office, not the USO!"

To which your eyes will seem to reply—with your own stare and a huge grin—"Lighten up, *Francis.*"

NOTES

Chapter One

Page 10   "An excited Kirt Womack of the Thiokol factory . . ." Matt Weinstein, *Managing to Have Fun* (New York: Simon & Schuster, 1997).

Page 20   "In a national study conducted by Harris Interactive, . . ." "U.S. Workers Reveal Which TV Bosses Remind Them of Their Own in New CareerBuilder.com Survey," CareerBuilder.com, July 25, 2007.

Page 22   "In 2005, researchers at the University of Maryland . . ." Michelle W. Murray, "Laughter Is the Best Medicine for Your Heart," UNM.com.

Page 23   "Dr. Lee Berk, assistant professor of family medicine . . ." Sinara Stull O'Donnell, 2004, "Laugh More at Work to Ease Office Stress," CareerJournal.com.

Page 23   "In a series of follow-up studies, . . ." "Planning to Watch a Comedy? It May Be

Good for You," University of California, Irvine, press release, November 13, 2001.

Page 26   "Studies on group decision making . . ." James K. Hazy, Jeffrey A. Goldstein, and Benyamin B. Lichtenstein, *Complex System Leadership Theory: New Perspectives from Complexity Science on Social and Organizational Effectiveness* (New York: ISCE Publishing, 2007).

Page 28   "Researchers Lawrence J. Peter and Bill Dana . . ." Lawrence Peter and Bill Dana, *The Laughter Prescription* (New York: Ballantine Books, 1987).

Page 31   "Of all the reasons . . ." Fabio Sala, "Laughing All the Way to the Bank," *Harvard Business Review*, September 2003.

Page 31   "A Hodge-Cronin & Associates . . ." R. Cronin, *Humor in the Workplace* (Rosemont, IL: Hodge-Cronin and Associates, 1997).

Page 31   "Survey of 737 chief executives . . ." Mary Rau-Foster, "Humor and Fun in the Workplace," Workplaceissues.com, June–July 2000.

Chapter Two

Page 40   "College students are more likely to recall a lecture . . ." Randy Garner, *College Teaching* 54, no. 1 (2006).

Page 46   "Humor was found to, 'facilitate . . ." C. M. Consalvo, "Humor in Management: No Laughing Matter," in *Humor: International*

Journal of Humor Research (New York: Monton de Gruyter, 1989).

Page 49　"Penn State University came to the same conclusion. . . ." John J. Sosik, Bruce J. Avolio, and Jane M. Howell. "A Funny Thing Happened on the Way to the Bottom Line," press release, May 20, 1996.

Page 56　"Many leaders follow the Zap Rule, . . ." Michael Kerr, "Speaking of Humor," mikekerr.com, 2006.

Chapter Three

Page 85　"The key to encouraging innovation . . ." "The importance of being Richard Branson," Knowledge@Wharton.com, January 12, 2005.

Page 86　"Here's a simple example of fun . . ." Leigh Buchanon, "That's Chief Entertainment Officer," *Inc. Magazine,* August 2007.

Page 87　"According to data published in the *Journal of Personality* . . ." A. M. Iser et al., "Positive Affect Facilitates Creative Problem Solving," *Journal of Personality and Social Psychology* (1987).

Page 92　"That's what Herb Kelleher, . . ." Kenneth Labich, "Is Herb Kelleher America's Best CEO?" *Fortune,* May 2, 1994.

Chapter Four

Page 107　"Virgin Group owner and founder Richard Branson . . ." "The importance of being

Richard Branson," Knowledge@Wharton .com, January 12, 2005.

Page 107 "According to a recent Sirota survey, . . ." "Employees Can't Get No Respect," clomedia.com, May 22, 2006.

Page 108 "'After 15 years as a physician executive,' . . ." David Ollier Weber, "Golden Rule and R-E-S-P-E-C-T Encourage Employee Loyalty," *Physician Executive,* July 2003.

Page 110 "Children laugh up to 400 times a day. . . ." Victor Rozek, "As I See It: Keep Laughing," ITJungle.com 13, no. 45 (2004).

Page 111 "10 Steps to Build . . ." Modified from Susan M. Heathfield, "How to Demonstrate Respect at Work," About.com: Human Resources.

Chapter Five

Page 113 "Norman Cousins's breakthrough research . . ." Norman Cousins, *Anatomy of an Illness as Perceived by the Patient* (New York: W. W. Norton, 1979).

Page 114 "A study of 2,015 Norwegians . . ." Marilyn Elias, "Study Links Sense of Humor, Survival." *United States Today,* March 13, 2007.

Page 116 "Humor scholar William Hampes . . ." William Hampes, "Relation between Humor and Empathic Concern," *Psychological Reports* 88 (2001): 241–244.

Page 118 "Participants of the study whose right . . ." "People with Brain Injury to Frontal

Lobe Don't Get Punch Lines: Prefer Slapstick Humor!" *Science Daily*, April 1, 1999.

Page 118 "A William M. Mercer survey . . ." Tom Stern, "Ten Ways to Inject Fun into the Workplace," FastCompany.com, February 16, 2007.

Page 119 "Research by Lee Berk, . . ." Sinara Stull O'Donnell, "Laugh More at Work to Ease Office Stress," CareerJournal.com, 2004.

Page 120 "According to a recent survey from Yankelovich, . . ." Richard Tait, "Let's Play," *Parade* magazine, July 30, 2006.

Page 121 "It helps children develop . . ." Gordon M. Burghardt, *The Genesis of Animal Play: Testing the Limits* (Cambridge, MA: MIT Press, 2005).

Page 121 "Being so addicted to portable devices . . ." "Think You Might Be Addicted to E-Mail? You're Not Alone," AOL press release, July 26, 2007.

Page 122 "California State University found that humor . . ." "Lighten Up," *Healthquest* newsletter, Warrenshepell.com.

Page 123 "Dr. Ashton Trice at Mary Baldwin College . . ." "Lighten Up," *Healthquest* newsletter, Warrenshepell.com.

Page 124 "There is a proven link between sense . . ." Anders Lindskov, "A Farewell to Clowns?" *Danmarks Paedagogiske Universitetsskole Quarterly Newsletter*, August 24, 2006.

Page 125 "'Humor and its partner laughter,' . . ." Steven M. Sultanoff, "Taking Humor

Seriously in the Workplace," Humormatters .com, 1993.

Chapter Six

Page 132 "3 in 10 workers . . ." "Employers and Employees: Making the Marriage Work," insightlink.com, based on a 2005 U.S. employee satisfaction survey.

Page 133 "Dr. David Abramis at California State University Long Beach . . ." Mary Rau-Foster, "Humor and Fun in the Workplace," Workplaceissues.com, June–July 2000.

Page 135 "A growing body of research . . ." Tom Still, "Laughing It Off," *Corporate Report Wisconsin*, August 1998.

Page 140 "Entertainment centers was around $8 million, . . ." Bryaian Deutschman, "The Enlightenment of Richard Branson," *Fast Company*, September 2006.

Page 141 "A survey of vice presidents and directors . . ." Heather Twidale, "Nowadays, Being 'Old Sourpuss' Is No Joke," *Working Woman*, March 1986.

Chapter Eight

Page 178 "We're a team of thousands . . ." "Quotes," Wikipedia.com.

Chapter Nine

Page 193 "A recent poll publicized by Ken Blanchard, . . ." James M. Kouzes and Barry

Z. Posner, *Encouraging the Heart* (San Francisco: Jossey-Bass, 2003).

Conclusion

Page 208 "Even the *Harvard Business Review* reports . . ." Fabio Sala, "Laughing All the Way to the Bank," *Harvard Business Review*, September 2003.

ABOUT THE AUTHORS

Adrian Gostick is the author of several very successful business books including the *New York Times, Wall Street Journal,* and *USA Today* best seller *The Carrot Principle.* He also wrote the best sellers *The Invisible Employee, A Carrot a Day,* and *The 24-Carrot Manager.* His work has been called a "must read for modern-day managers" by Larry King of CNN, "fascinating" by *Fortune,* and "admirable" and "startling" by the *Wall Street Journal.* Adrian's books have been translated into 20 languages and are sold in more than 50 countries around the world. As workplace researcher, author, and presenter, he has appeared on network television programs and has been quoted in dozens of business publications and magazines. Adrian earned a master's degree in Strategic Communication and Leadership from Seton Hall University, where he is a guest lecturer on organizational culture. He lives with his wife and son in the Rocky Mountains. You can reach him at adrian@levityeffect.com.

Philosopher. Humanitarian. *People* magazine's "Sexiest Man Alive." Author and lecturer **Scott Christopher** would like to meet the guy who is all those things. A self-described corporate outsider—having worked many years in the make-believe world of television and film—Scott now travels the world speaking to standing-room-only audiences about building engaging workplace cultures. Rejoining the workaday world, Scott discovered a yawning divide between people who want success and those who actually get it. He discovered the chasm can be bridged with levity. A Harvard MBA and a PhD from Princeton are two important-sounding degrees. Scott got his bachelor's degree from Brigham Young University. His energy and engaging wit make for unforgettable speeches and seminars that touch hearts and split sides. A regular humor columnist for *Workplace HR* magazine, author of *Lighten Up,* and contributing author of the best-selling book *A Carrot A Day,* Scott also finds the time to spend with his wife Liz and five sons. You can reach him at scott@levityeffect.com.

LEARN MORE AT LEVITYEFFECT.COM

If you want a hilarious, motivating keynote speech or workshop for your organization, please click on this link www.levityeffect.com. Gotcha. It's still a book. But if you go to our web site you'll find unforgettable training that helps you:

- Enhance fun at work
- Build trust
- Create dynamic presentations that sell
- Hold more effective meetings
- Enhance creativity
- Create a great workplace

While on our web site, you can find great levity moments from history, more opening jokes for your next speech, and a hundred other ways to lighten up your workplace.